MEMORIES OF A CHRISTIAN ADVENTURER

MEMORIES OF A CHRISTIAN ADVENTURER

HUNTER, PREACHER, GLOBETROTTER

"Through many dangers, toils and snares
I have already come"

AUTOBIOGRAPHY OF
JOHN HITCHCOCK

iUniverse LLC
Bloomington

MEMORIES OF A CHRISTIAN ADVENTURER
Hunter, Preacher, Globetrotter

iUniverse books may be ordered through booksellers or by contacting:

iUniverse LLC
1663 Liberty Drive
Bloomington, IN 47403
www.iuniverse.com
1-800-Authors (1-800-288-4677)

ISBN: 978-1-4917-1484-3 (sc)
ISBN: 978-1-4917-1483-6 (hc)
ISBN: 978-1-4917-1482-9 (e)

Library of Congress Control Number: 2013920836

Printed in the United States of America.

iUniverse rev. date: 01/10/2014

"About John Hitchcock"

The Story of my Life, Memories of a Christian Adventurer ("The Story") reads like a great fictional book, but it is not fiction. It is the true story of a remarkable individual, whose quest for adventure and travel is blended with his greater love—his friendship with God.

Imagine combining the traits of a Crocodile Dundee with that of an evangelist into the same person. Such a man was John Hitchcock.

In his biography John tells his story, or rather *stories* which combine into his one big unique story. Each story is neatly packaged into single successive chapters. The reading of one chapter leaves the reader with a sense of awe and a desire to read the next. What begins as relaxed reading soon accelerates into a rush to see what happens next.

John's story has as a backdrop of not only the bustling city life of the greater Johannesburg of the 1940s and 50s, but also of the wild bush lands of outback Africa. John's story starts as a little boy living in the shadows of the gigantic sand heaps of Johannesburg's mining industry.

It is here where he inherits a severe speech impediment *alalia syllabaris,* (stuttering) after suffering from meningitis. John shares his difficulty trying to relate to his childhood peers, all the time inhibited by his *stammering, lisping tongue.* The reader feels his pain and is reminded of the difficulties that such and other individuals with other handicaps experience.

Then John experiences what some may describe as a supernatural encounter. In a blissful moment, which he describes as the *baptism in the Holy Spirit,* John encounters that mysterious experience of *glossolalia*—ecstatic speech—the speaking in other tongues.

John describes his personal and private spiritual rebirth—on his knees by the radio, as he listens to the world renowned evangelist Billy Graham and the singing of George Beverly Shea.

But before all of this there was John's love for sports. In spite of his stutter, or perhaps because of it, John excels in his sports activities. He excels in almost everything he tries—rugby, boxing, wrestling—even once engaging the Natal provincial champion.

John reminisces on his love for the wild, for nature and for animals. Story after story captivates the reader's attention. The reader will smile when John's childhood pet monkey *Choppy Adams* leaps into the story and then later *Bossie* the mongoose. And the story about the baboon in one of John's big game hunting trips is hilarious. And many more . . . But not all is humor. Big game hunting is dangerous.

If cats have nine lives, John has ninety-nine. While others wisely avoid it, John seems to revel walking as close to the edge of life as possible. Page after page is filled with some nail biting accounts of sharks and lions, buffalo and elephants, and the reader is amazed that John could have somehow escaped death so many times.

Some of these hair-raising encounters become blended with John's faith and friendship with God. For example, John becomes infected with an incurable disease during one of his crocodile hunting expeditions. Yet faith in God causes him to triumph and medical technology proves that he is in fact cured. While it is inexplicable to medical science, John gives God the credit.

While reading *The Story* the reader begins to catch a glimpse of the passions hidden in the soul of the man. John seems to be passionate about sports, hunting and travel. But these are but natural parallels of a deeper passion—his love for his God and the Gospel.

Though his speech remained impeded by a stutter in his everyday life, his tongue was released to speak every time *the anointing*—that influence of the Holy Spirit came upon him. What seems to be a stark contradiction becomes a fresh miracle every time he opens his mouth to speak God's Word. The stutterer becomes the anointed preacher.

John recounts how he and his wife and children travel by air and land to spread the Message they believe in the most, and the adventure continues. When he mounts the public platform, the rugged adventurer is transformed into a well groomed clergyman, but different. With the same passion he displays in everyday life, the message of the old rugged cross and the power of the Spirit that had freed him flows from his lips.

The Story of My Life—Memories of a Christian Adventurer will not only benefit you with good entertaining reading, but perhaps spark within you that same fire of life and of God: your story, your life, your adventure . . .

Evangelist Dr. Joel Hitchcock

CONTENTS

Dedication

I dedicate this book to my dear wife, Cornelia and our four closest children, Galilee, Evangeline, Charlene and Johnson.

Important note

This book is written in chronological order by date and year and therefore the events do not follow in harmony.

Linguistic terminology is written in South African custom and could therefore differ from American English.

All quotations from the Bible are from the King James Version unless otherwise stated.

Acknowledgements

I express my sincere gratitude to my dear wife, Cornelia for spending months of hours in the preparation of the manuscript of this book. She did all the typing, editing, insertion of photo's, etc., As it was a first for both her and myself we were helped step by step to cross every hurdle by my nephew, Evangelist Dr Joel Hitchcock who also designed the covers. Sincere thanks to both.

INTRODUCTION

Reviewing my life, I confer that it has been more than interesting. In fact, my life has been colored with the pen of the Master's skillful and creative design. My life's story is filled with great excitement and many, many dramas.

Many of the following stories have been used in my sermons throughout the years; and people have often asked me to put pen to paper in order to make it available for others to enjoy.

Nothing about my life has ever been "ordinary." My life experiences have been nothing less than one big adventure! I have been privileged to see and do almost everything I thought would be interesting, surely I have come through the fire and through the waters of life and am alive to tell my story!

So, here goes, if you're ready to read it, I am finally ready to tell it . . . .

This is the story of my life; hence the excessive usage of the personal pronoun "I" as life is self-centered in all aspects. It is noteworthy that the letter "I" lies square in the middle of the word SIN. Strange as it may seem, my greatest enemy in life, the person I fear most is my own self.

Life has its ups and downs, its con-caves and con-vexes. Life's graph is forever in motion. We, as personalities live in the most variable and changing environment which govern our mortal lives. You and I are in motion; there is no bridling the chariot, and our pulses beat the funeral march to the tomb! Everyone would gladly remember his victories—and apexes, but alas, the ghosts of memory still haunt our minds and we are forced to remember and so often call to mind our defeats and embarrassments. In this little epoch of my life I plan to portray both the defeats and victories—I thus ask you to cry with me in the mires of despair and laugh and frolic with me in the heights of victory. Every story that is listed in the following pages is true. I have not exaggerated in the victories neither eliminated in the defeats, I leave it as it is, and if at any time you feel that I have leaned a little toward the course of imagination, please be assured, that every word is true. Your life and mine is molded by uncountable elements and factors such as environment, genetic inheritance, upbringing, love, discipline, habits, parents, and so on. Some play greater rolls than others. In my own life two most important factors have governed my life. I feel that above all other these two played the greatest importance in what I've done and what I've achieved. The first is a severe speech impediment and the second is my personal encounter with the Lord Jesus Christ.

Let's then go to the annals of my mind and draw out the files and taste the bitter and the sweet.

Some men seem to easily blend in with a monotonous "every day the same" life. I was born "wild at heart" and need variety. Perhaps I was not born this way, but rather it was cultivated by the strictness of my dad's discipline. Overdue restraint of freedom can sometimes have a devastating effect and tend to divert a desired path into an opposite direction.

Life opened its doors to me on December 23rd, 1939 in Germiston, South Africa where I was born to Dyason Roland and Beatrix Cornelia Hitchcock. It seems as if in life's game of chess the first move was "odds against me" for this date resulted in only one gift for birthday and Christmas. However, the second was greatly in my favor for it was my privilege to be honored by great, yet strict parents. There is one certain law in life and that is "as you sow, so you will reap." My folks have always sowed in integrity, honesty and humility and they have certainly reaped the same in life. Some upper hand has blessed them.

My Dad and Mom

Any clear thinking individual will have to admit that there are two forces forever in a violent clash, in, and about and for his life. It would seem as if sinister spiritual forces are forever striving to accomplish their will within us. These forces are good and evil, righteous and unrighteous.

My life was pretty normal until the age of three, when I was struck down by the feared disease of meningitis. I am told that during these years, very few victims survived this disease. My dad, although not a dedicated, born-again Christian, prayed earnestly and a peace and revelation came to him that I would be OK. However, OK best describes this situation because although surviving the disease, I was left with a horrendous stutter, which would grossly affect the rest of my life, for good and bad. No one who possesses the gift of free speech can even begin to imagine the pure hell that a stutterer has to endure. Who would understand the intense fear associated with the act of opening your mouth to talk? Not to mention the embarrassment when cruel jokes were told to the laughing glee of all that are present. There remains tremendous embarrassment, haunting memories, missed opportunities associated with this cruel handicap. If meningitis was the cause of my stammering tongue I shall never know but my parents tell me that since this occasion I started stuttering. This stammer however, did not hinder me until my school days when I found that I could not speak as others. A vicious cycle began to set in. It's difficult to determine which the leading factor is, but one leads to the other. A loss of confidence leads to fear which in turn leads to a tension of throat, nerves and muscles which in turn leads to a loss of confidence. This severe stutter was destined to play an enormous roll in my life. How well do I remember the times of embarrassment resulting from this speech impediment? It occasioned others to look upon me as one of the simpler types in life. It resulted in an inferiority complex. I remember how in 6th grade I had to stand and read back my test mark in class. As always when I had to say something an awful fear began to envelop me. I would think the sentence out beforehand, would start substituting words, words which would be easier to say than others. As always when the time came to speak I would be so nervous and tensed that my jaw locked, my face started twitching, my eyes would close tightly and I would start spitting. My mark was twenty-nine and a half, but I just could not say it. I tried for a full five minutes. The kind teacher tried to relax me which of course only added to my utter discomfort being embarrassed in front of the whole class. I finally burst into tears and the boy next to me had to read back my mark. How simple it was for him just to say twenty-nine and a half. This experience repeated itself innumerable times every day of my life.

In grade 12 I had to say the word "co-tan"—a symbol used in trigonometry. It just would not come out! The teacher started to mock me saying that I should imagine myself out on the play field asking somebody for a coke, and then just substitute the word "co-tan". It just would not come! Again I started crying (at the age of eighteen) and sat down. The teacher asked me what I would do if it was my future boss. *"God, I wish I knew,"* I thought.

Back in grade 5, the teacher asked a difficult question and offered the handsome sum of two shillings and sixpence to the child who knew the answer. I knew it but did not have the moral courage to answer.

Years after I graduated I had the rather comical experience of having started work at a new company. One morning I came in the door and started upstairs. Whilst going up the managing director came down. He greeted me with a cheerful "good morning John." It came so unexpected upon me that the "Good morning Sir" only came out when I was upstairs around the corner and he downstairs, out of the door. Rather comical—yes, but at the time most embarrassing. Of course I lacked the courage to go to him and tell him why I did not greet him. Under those pressurizing circumstances I would of course never be able to complete the sentence. I was trying to tell a joke once to my friends during break at school. They had to forfeit their whole play time waiting for me to finish. Half way through I wished that I had never commenced. The bell rang when I was almost through—they never did hear the end of the joke!

Then there is forever the cruel, unthinking person who always has a joke to tell about the stutterer. I often wondered if these wretches had pumpkin pips instead of brains. I must have heard the parachute joke a hundred times. Perhaps I can tell it now at some other stutters' expense. I've had my times of embarrassment. A guy jumped out of an airplane and had to count to ten before pulling the ripcord. He finally came out of a haystack counting t-t-t-ten.

The stammer however, also did have its benefits. It taught me to be able to use myself. Although a puny-thin fellow I always seemed to be the best fighter in the class. At grade 5 I was champion of the school and could smash any kid in 7th grade. I took up boxing as a kid. Nobody ever did try to harm me by harassing me. He would have come off second best. Those who did tell jokes at my expense—did it unthinking. I just laughed with the rest whilst covering up awful embarrassment.

Fortunately I was gifted with the will power to overcome. While I was academically handicapped, I did excel at any sport and received numerous accolades in boxing, soccer, rugby, cricket, tennis, swimming and diving. While the stutter caused a timid, inferiority complex in my mind and spirit, my body's ability to produce excelled, and three years before sixth grade, I was the champion fighter at school. Nobody tried to bully me, either physically or emotionally. A challenge became my "piece of cake."

Another sad effect of stuttering was that I was unable to be a sweet smooth talker. I was never able to make it with the opposite sex and up to today, I'm still thankful that I was sent to a boys' school. The embarrassment of my school years would have been too compounded by having girls in class. As mentioned before many times in class, when called upon to say something and a word would not come out, I would break down in tears. While trying to utter a word, my face would contort into a barrage of face pulling, blinking of eyes, knees lifting, spitting, etc. etc. so I am thankful that there were no girls in my high school years. It was shear hell! I do sincerely believe that I was the worst stutterer to ever walk Planet Earth.

As the purpose of my life was destined by God to become a healing Pentecostal evangelist, it is doubtless that my stutter would play a crucial part in this ministry. After all, how could one who feared to talk in front of two or more ever wish and hope to address crowds of scores, hundreds and thousands. How could such a one ever talk on radio or TV? Well, with God, all things are possible. I have heard how that God touched the tongues of great preachers like Oral Roberts, Lorne Fox, Benny Hinn, etc., and in one split second, they were set free, but in my case, it was not so. Even today at age 73 I still stutter badly but the great miracle comes when I pray, preach or prophecy, I am not only "stutter free", but also gifted with a great gift of eloquence. In fact, the easiest way of all for me to speak is when I speak in tongues (*1Cor 14*). It is then when I do not have to stumble through the unseen, mind movie of letters, but rather just flow by the Spirit's utterance.

1953

In memoir of Tjoppie Adams

This book would not be complete if my buddy Mr. Tjoppie Adams was not mentioned. You see Tjoppie Adams was a Vervet monkey, and he spent sixteen years in close companionship with me. I caught him at the age of thirteen and he shared my years till I was twenty-nine. Blind in one eye, I could never make out his sex, perhaps a female—perhaps a freak of nature. I will refer to it as him. Tjoppie shared my feelings of defeat and joy. He slept with me every night in the cold winters. Weekends we would loosen him from his pole and he would tour the streets of Primrose-Germiston where he became well acquainted with the neighborhood and often shared a meal at their table. After my ex-wife and I returned from honeymoon and slept in my old bed, she awoke the morning to find Tjoppie sitting on her chest looking at her. Needless to say a wife will never share her husband with another woman and Tjoppie had to move out. I always feared the day that Tjoppie would die. Fortunately it came an easy way. He had to live with people on acreage while my dad was sent to Luanda; Angola as manager of South African Airways for three months. During this time Tjoppie got loose and till today I have never seen Tjoppie again. It was better this way. The Member of Parliament of Germiston lived behind us and in later years when his sons opened a panel beating/body shop business and decided on a name for it, they titled it with the grand name of "Tjoppie Adams Panel Beaters."

An intense love for animals has always dominated my character and I have been the proud owner of a monkey, two bush babies, an owl, hawk, eagles, a crow, a mongoose, guinea pigs, rabbits, a crocodile, Etcetera.

My Vervet Monkey Pet

1955

Wrestling the Natal Champion

Being about seventeen years of age I had shortly before taken up a wrestling career. I probably had one or two lessons. Suffice it to say I was absolutely and totally a "rookie." If I knew the basic full or half nelson, that would have been the utmost. All I can remember is "get behind your opponent to the side, grip the opposite wrist. Get your arm under his arm, role him over, pin him on the floor and keep him there for the count. That's the half nelson and that's all I knew."

It was vacation time and two of my friends and I had a holiday planned at Durban, near the beach. So with Jimmy Butts, Herby Pinkham and I we caught the train and was received by uncle Ronny Boshoff, Jimmy's uncle.

Uncle Ronny was a "Springbok" South African wrestling champion and we were immediately invited to the training courses. Neither Jimmy nor Herby wrestled but they began bragging to uncle Ronny about me, so I was quickly matched with an opponent. Apparently I didn't do too bad and so was drafted to wrestle the Natal champion on the following Saturday night. This was definitely the last thing I desired. I had certainly not come on holiday to wrestle, keep fit and jog. I had come to smoke, lie on the beach and perhaps meet a girl. I was now under stress which gyrated to higher levels when I was informed that my bout would be in a packed Durban City Hall, and it would be the main bout after interval. Oh man, I still groan within!

To gain more interest and obviously collection entrance money an advertising hype was generated stating that a very special opponent had come down all the way from the Transvaal to challenge their beloved, undefeated, Natal, Olympic candidate.

On arriving at the packed City Hall, I quickly gained knowledge of the great expectation fight just after interval. Had I known the Lord at that time, I would greatly have anticipated and prayed for the rapture. "Lord, have mercy tonight!"

During interval and as I came into the ring my friends brought the house down by shouting; "Jo'burg!-Jo'burg!" The opposition responded with the chant; "Durban Natal!—Durban Natal!" The chant became a deafening roar and seemed endless! And there I stood in my corner with shaking knees, feeling as lonely as never before! Opposite me I viewed my opponent with bulging biceps, muscles and all, scrutinizing me like a "wrecking yard dog!" To enhance my fear and his reputation, he only had one eye, apparently having lost the other in wrestling. When the ill-fated bell rang and we engaged, I only knew two things. Get behind him and apply the half nelson or be sure to slip out of any grip that he tried on me. The latter was probably all that was accomplished and I am relieved to report that the three rounds ended amongst much applause in his favor by a point's decision. At least I was not pinned. I later continued my wrestling career and did become a more accomplished wrestler until God saved me at eighteen years of age, at which time I forfeited all my sports careers. I rolled my trophies of boxing, wrestling, diving, swimming, rugby and tennis at the feet of the King of Kings and Lord of Lords to do His sovereign will. I still held onto only one—cigarettes and tobacco.

Myself as a young Boxer

My remarkable brother Tony

I was privileged to share my years with an unforgettable character named Tony. Whilst a child he had a pair of ears that earned him the nickname of "Ou Haas"—Haas means rabbit in Afrikaans. I've always called him this. What I lacked in speech, Tony had a natural gift with. He seemed to talk his way into everything he wanted. A dynamic character he possesses has resulted in him being a very well-known and well liked character. A Lieutenant at the age of twenty-six in the South African Police force, he was transferred to Bureau of state security and made his mark there.

Tony had one weakness, and that was a swift striking blow of his well-formed and powerful arm. Will I ever forget the incident when the manager of the mess at the mine where I worked in Phalaborwa revealed his usual pig-manners! I had on previous occasions taken some guests to the mine mess to have a meal and every time I was embarrassed by this man's manners. Unfortunately for him "Ou Haas" came along. We had no sooner settled down to our meal when a voice shouted from the back saying—Tell that man to get his child's pram out of the isle. Tony removed the carry cot with his few months old child in and put it beneath the table and wheeled the pram into the foyer. At that moment the principal men from the mine came in. They consisted of Director, Managers and guests from the United States of America. They were served with beers. Tony wanted a beer, and when he was told by the waiter that he was not allowed one, his temperature soured higher. He got up and walked to the mess manager and demanded to know why he could not have a beer. Tony was chased to his seat. He was shivering all over with anger. At that moment Mr. Pig-manners came along and whilst he had his finger poked in Tony's nose he unfortunately kicked the carry cot and the child, Joel Hitchcock was disturbed. This of course was too much for Tony. The manager was sent sprawling over the neatly decorated tables by a powerful punch. When he stumbled, Tony was there to get his moneys' worth. Needless to say he became as timid as a mouse and begged for mercy. Tony looks somewhat like me and when I got back to work, I found myself fired. It took some doing to try and explain that it was not me but an unforgettable character named Tony.

Both Tony and I played rugby from our earliest days. We both played for our schools' first team and later played club rugby. I positioned at fly half and full back whilst Tony favored scrum half and center. I found myself a talented kicker and even today at 72 years of age I can still dropkick and kick a torpedo (like Americans throw a ball, a football) with both left and right feet.

I played club rugby for no more than a year after leaving school and just as I was chosen to represent a Transvaal sub union game which might have led me to great heights in a career of rugby, I sacrificed my rugby career to God. I rolled my talent at the feet of the King desiring rather to excel in His work.

Tony however went on to great heights and whilst he and his dear wife Elaine were stationed in England he captained the London Springboks for four years. He also played for Twickenham, Wanderers and Middlesex counties. He followed well in our dad's career that played scrum half for both Orange Free State and Transvaal provinces (two of the four states of South Africa.) Dad would doubtlessly have played for the famous Springbok team if he were not called away to the Second World War. Before the war he however did play Springbok trials and succumbed against the famous Danie Craven (Mr. Rugby.)

Tony also partook in a lot of boxing being active from age seven to twenty two. Today Tony and Elaine are the proud parents of four children who all serve God. Joel and Jessica are flaming evangelists, Johnny Boy does construction and Jolene is mother of three most beautiful daughters and one son.

Tony and Elaine

Taxidermy—My gratifying hobby

Ever since a child I've been an avid bird lover, so it was no wonder that I wanted my room full of them, and so my taxidermy hobby began at a very young age.

First I had to acquire a rifle. For some reason my parents never bought Tony and I anything. We always had to acquire them ourselves and so it was that I did any odd jobs to obtain some money. I specifically remember accumulating Coca Cola bottles which I would sell for recycling. I thus built up my little piggy bank account and it was a very happy day when I was able to purchase a used B.S.A

(Birmingham Small Arms) #1 pellet gun. I'd have preferred#2, but that was definitely out of reach. I still remember riding home on my bike and singing, "Thank you Jesus for giving me this rifle" on the tune of "*Thank you Jesus for saving my soul.*" I was so glad. I was about fourteen years of age, and this day was the commencement of many days of excitement, adventure and contentment.

After subscribing to a taxidermy mail course, I received my materials from the Northwest School of Taxidermy in America. It was the year of 1954.

While my friends were venturing into drugs, I felt content to spend my time hunting birds, in a nearby grove of poplar trees. Let it be stated emphatically that this, my area of Primrose, Germiston, South Africa was no favorite haunt of the many beautiful species of birds found in South Africa. It could certainly be called a "poverty stricken bird watchers paradise." So I had to be content with what I could get but after much practice the walls and ceiling of my room began to be graced with many birds.

One day I shot an extremely prized trophy. It was a "Black Shouldered Kite." I was so eager to add this hawk to my collection but when I went to pick it up it was still very much alive and dug its vicious claws deep into my hand. My shot had broken its wing. I now decided to keep it, mend its wound and perhaps try training it to do falconry. To feed it, proved to be a major obstacle so every day I went to the poplar bushes and acquired a turtle dove, mouse, or rat for its meal.

I hated school and it was a very easy matter for my will to be conquered by a "playing hooky" or locally known as a "bunk school" spirit. I would slip my rifle under my trousers with the bend of the rifle at my knee. The barrel went into my shoe and the butt under my school blazer under my arm pit. Next stop would be matches and a few of Mom's "Cavalla Cigarettes." After fear of being detected, I would greet my parents, head for the bus stop, only to exit down the road and head for the "Poppies" (poplar bushes.)

When the hawk's wound seemed mended, I decided to set it free and launched it into the air. Sad to say, the wing snapped in midair and it plummeted to the ground. After these weeks, I had given it a name so I walked to inspect "Pete Hawk's" new dilemma, and found the wing to be totally severed. I clipped it off with a scissors and now I had a pet as a permanent asset. I wrapped some tape around the handlebars of my bike and Pete Hawk accompanied me every day where I went—mainly to the swimming baths where I loved diving more than bathing and swimming. I was able to do many dives with grace and beauty. Naming them would be "The Swallow dive, The Pike, Forward and back somersaults and from the High board, I could do the Milberg, one and a half and two and a half somersaults. During these years there was animosity between English and Afrikaans speaking kids and frequent fights would be the order of the day. Thirteen years later when I met Pastor Tinus Cronje and during the course of our many conversations I mentioned my affiliation with Pete Hawk. As he had attended the Afrikaans school nearby my English school, he was amazed to hear that I was the much feared and talked about Englishmen amongst his Afrikaans friends as I had acquired the reputation and legend of the guy who had a hawk bodyguard and would fling it in the face of any Afrikaans foe!

My taxidermy hobby grew and later having moved to the low veld of South Africa my walls were graced by a Lions head, and many species of antelope. I shot and mounted the biggest Cape buffalo head I had ever set eyes on. When I saw the world record which still today hangs in the bar of the Hectorspruit/Malelane Hotel, I was amazed to know that my Buffalo Trophy was far superior.

I had the privilege of mounting the world record lions head. This lion was very old and killed a hundred and forty seven of the farmer's beef stock. He was very desperate to shoot this lion. On a day this lion jumped out of the grass a few yards ahead of me, but I could not get in a shot as the tracker was in front of me. The farmer finally shot it and it measured out eleven foot six inches from snout to tail. This is still the world record lion today, but has never been officially listed. Whilst skinning this lion there was a tremendous bruise on the hind leg and one of the workers said he saw the lion attacking a male buffalo and was severely hurt in the attack.

The world record lion as mounted by myself

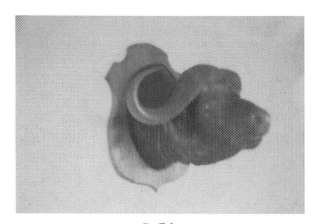

Buffalo

During my years of work I still maintained my hobby and later opened my own business named "Safari Taxidermists" which I ran together with crocodile hunting. My life's work prior to the ministry was:

1. Excise Officer with the South African Customs and Excise.
2. Accountant at 3M Company.
3. Shop Clerk at Jan Smuts—now Oliver Tambo International Airport. Before entering the ministry in August 1969 I moved to Phalaborwa in 1966 and worked as an accountant at the Water board and later done shift work at Phalaborwa Mining Company.

Once entered into the ministry as an evangelist and moving from city to city, house to house, my treasured collection of trophies quickly became damaged and obsolete and so ended a period of fifteen years.

1958

My born-again Experience

The day and hour of September 16, 1958, South African time, ticked on the clock. It was a Tuesday night. During the past night's, I had been reading the famed inspired book by John Bunyan written from Bedford Prison England in years gone by. I had read this book before and it seemed like a lot of "gibberish" to me, however, now the Spirit of God was revealing the wonderful truths and this book was now being used as a mighty tool of God in my "soon to come" salvation. I had just reached the Interval chapter. The clock struck 10.00 pm and as I had been listening to the radio preaching of Billy Graham in these years, on his *"Hour of decision"* I tuned in again. Due to the strict influence of the Calvinist Dutch Reformed Church orientated government, no religious broadcasts by any other religion were allowed in South Africa. Nevertheless, Dr. Billy Grahams' shortwave broadcast came in loud and clear from Lourenco Marques, the capital of Portuguese dominated Mozambique. While huddling around the old radio, Billy Graham concluded his message and George Beverly Shea sang "I've wandered far away from God, now I'm Coming Home." It must have been 10.27 pm sharp and then it happened!

Oh, my Lord, and how it happened! The presence of God filled the room. I said to God, "Lord, I do not have much to offer you—only five loaves and two fishes. But here is my life—I give it to you."

Suddenly the presence of God moved not only in the room but into my heart. My heart was strangely warmed, my eyes became a fountain of tears and I became "a new creation in Christ Jesus." I was gloriously "born again!" The burden of sin lifted; a sweet peace and jubilee came over me. The former John Hitchcock died that minute and a new John took his place. 105 Barbara Road, Germiston, South Africa is the place of death and resurrection. My life turned around. The pendulum had reached its zenith and now started its opposite course. Though stuttering, I tried to tell all my friends of my experience and decision, and that God loved them too. Some cut company, others drifted into indifference, but God gave me the greatest company of new friends.

The old radio where I was saved

My parents were not churchgoing individuals and hence, I never went. However, my parents did insist that we go to Sunday school as children and I do recall one experience which may have led to my born-again experience in later years. I was approximately twelve years of age and attended Sunday school at a little Baptist meeting in my school hall. Having missed one meeting, I was told by a friend at school the next day that he had accepted the Lord as his Savior at Sunday school. I still recall the disappointment I felt and had remorse that I had not been present. The following Sunday, however, I did approach the teacher and requested him to pray the sinner's prayer with me. I believe God saw my heart that day and although I did not receive the inward experience that day, I do believe God scheduled it at the right time.

1959

Deliverance from nicotine

Soon after my born-again experience, I developed an immense hunger and passion to preach the word of God and become an evangelist. One obstacle constantly blocked my way. It was smoking. I began to smoke at age twelve and I was now almost nineteen years of age.

The Holy Ghost was now convicting me of smoking so I decided to give it up. Little did I know how difficult this was to fulfill. I had already made a full consecration to God which included forfeiting an illustrious rugby career so cigarettes were my last bastion. Well do I remember one morning en route to catch the bus to work when the Holy Spirit said to me: "John you will never grow and get further in your spiritual life until you overcome the addiction." So, I did try to quit on numerous occasions. To aggravate my problem was that as an Excise Officer I was granted the privilege of stocking my inventory with any amount and types of cigarettes and tobacco so I had already acquired a cupboard full of my favorite types. This cupboard was approximately 3'x4'x5' so into the distant future my habit would cost me nothing, and I still had the privilege of a never ending supply.

Many times as I would try to quit the habit, as it happened as the hour struck five to eleven am, I would succumb and open another pack. I recall one evening coming home from my girlfriend and the Spirit of God confronted me as I entered the back porch. God inquired: "What about your smoking John?" To which I answered and said: "God I've tried. Frankly and honestly, I cannot give up. I am bound, addicted, I am a slave," but your Word states:

"And ye shall know the truth, and the truth shall make you free." (John 8:32) "If the Son therefore shall make you free, ye shall be free indeed." (John 8:36)

So God, I said, "it's not my job to set myself free, it's yours—You do it in your own time." I now relaxed in the peace of God.

A few nights later I attended a meeting conducted by a young and flaming evangelist named Rueben van Eijk. Rueben happened to be my cousin as our mothers were sisters. I'll never forget the sermon he preached. It was based on

"There shall in no wise enter into it (heaven) anything that defileth." *(Revelation 21:27)*

Again, I was under heavy conviction and at the close of the meeting I asked Rueben to pray for my deliverance. I then resolved to enjoy my last smoke and take up the battle again—tomorrow trying to get past 10:55 am. My last smoke was a "Texan" cigarette.

Morning came and my first smoke was normally on the bus, but I had no desire to smoke. I didn't even think about it. Eleven o'clock past into lunch hour and I experienced no craving. "Knock off" time came and on the train and bus home, I still had no craving. After a week passed with hardly a thought I suppose I realized that God had set me free. I have never smoked again but during the years had many dreams that I would take one draw and be enslaved all over again. Needless to say I wouldn't even light a cigarette for anybody. I was made totally free that night in November 1959. Health wise I was fortunate. My brother Tony, three years younger than I, was not so fortunate. He smoked all the years until last year 2011. He has suffered a heart attack, a quadruple bypass and three cancer operations. I believe a third of his bladder was removed. We prayed much, he gave up smoking and today he is cancer free. *Thank you God!* It was shortly after this that I received the baptism of the Holy Ghost and fire.

My baptism in the Holy Spirit

I was raised Methodist, and do remember the fear I experienced during confirmation class. Upon commencement, the plus/minus twenty children had to state their names in turn. Needless to say, the fear and nervousness blocked any word which I tried to utter. My name would not come out and I finally gave up. Every day experiences like this left me with a tremendous inferiority complex. This was due to change radically. Jesus said,

"You shall receive power after the Holy Ghost comes upon you," (Acts 1:8) "Tarry in the City of Jerusalem until ye be endued with power from on high." (Luke 24:49)

Some weeks after my conversion, I saw an advertisement in the newspaper. It stated "Inspired singing, inspired preaching." Next Sunday, I found this church. It happened to be a Church of God. During service, someone in the pews began to talk loudly in tongues. I did not understand what was happening. However, Jesus said, "My sheep know my voice." No one had to tell me that this was of God. I just knew it and knew that I had to have it. I was hungry for God and having found a church which was alive and on fire, I never returned to Methodism. So began a time of sacrificing many petty things in my life, two of which were rugby and smoking. With all my heart, I began to seek the baptism of the Holy Ghost.

I understood according to many scriptures in the book of Acts, chiefly Acts 2:1-4, that when one receives the baptism of the Holy Ghost, it would be accompanied by the miraculous sign of tongues and/or prophecy. At this time, God had joined me with a number of friends, all of whom were hungry for the infilling/baptism of the Holy Ghost.

Our Pastor had set Tuesday nights apart to pray for candidates who sought this experience and so we came expectantly. That night four of my friends received this wonderful experience. When it came my turn for prayer and hands were laid upon me, I experienced liquid warmth in the pit of my stomach. It welled up to my tongue and I knew I had to speak. Sadly, again the fear of talking in front of people invaded my mind and I clamped up. Needless to say, I left church that night very disappointed. However, having always been a fighter, I set my mind to receive it the next week.

The next Tuesday when the pastor laid his hands on me, I did not feel the liquid heat but my faith was geared to accept. A loud gushing torrent of sound flowed from my mouth and best of all, there was no stutter whatsoever. I was talking plainly. In conjunction with this miracle, I was instantly delivered from my inferiority complex. The lamb had turned into a lion. Not long after this, we began conducting street meetings. I began testifying on the streets and lo and behold, to my utter surprise, every time I shared my testimony or preached, I was totally fluent. There was no stammer. As stated before, to this day, I still stutter in the natural, but every time I pray, talk in tongues, prophesy or preach, I am totally fluent, not just fluent, but also eloquent. Truly, God's strength is made perfect in our weakness and therefore, Paul writes and states, *"When I am weak, then am I strong."* God joined me with several friends and for several years our time was spent praying, preaching and doing whatever we could for God. I painted signs on bridges, mine dumps, etc. I distributed thousands of tracts. Our street meetings continued for seven years, five times per week. Eleven years after I got saved, I stepped out into full time ministry. It was August 1969.

1963-1967

The "Awake Jesus Cometh"—mine dump

Some four years after my dramatic meeting with Jesus, and being so zealously "on fire" for God, I decided to venture into a full time ministry for God. This decision was however premature. I resigned my job and did anything I could for God.

I began with a hitchhiking trip down to the forests of Knysna where I spent some weeks fasting and praying. Upon my return to the "Rand" I began painting signs on bridges, rocks, and any place where the public was likely to see them. I still feel this ministry today for it has been said that "the pen is mightier than the tongue." I distributed thousands of tracks. On a note of humor, whilst I was working as an Excise Officer and been stationed in the liquor producing factories, I would sit along the conveyer belts pasting Bible verses on the passing liquor bottles. Sometime later my boss called me into his office and severely reprimanded me. I can just imagine how someone went to a liquor store; purchased his favorite brandy and when he sat down to enjoy it was faced with a convicting Bible verse.

South Africa is gold country producing some 90% of the worlds and 70% of the West's gold. Thus it is no wonder that the White Waters reef have so many mines and yes, so many mine dumps. They have always been a "pain to the eye." Fortunately the mining companies began recycling them and thus reclaimed an innumerable financial value in gold and land.

The mine dumps being mostly composed of sludge which upon drying turned into a fine sand likened unto sea sand. One dump however, near where I lived, had a wall of black rocks consisting of one to two feet square. This represented a "golden" opportunity to paint a sign for Jesus. I began planning such an event, and decided on the phrase: "AWAKE—JESUS IS COMING!"

The face of this "rock strewn" dump (a better word would be hill or mountain) was almost vertical being about a 70 to 80% incline. The dump itself would be approximately 1800 feet high (550 meters.) I decided to paint the letters 45 feet high and 3 feet wide (41 x 2.7 meters.) I couldn't afford paint so I decided to use "white wash", and the only way to get it up there would be to carry it up in a 5 gallon open bucket. One letter required 8 buckets to complete, thus 16 letters required 128 climbs up and down the mine dump. 128 Climbs up an 80 degree incline on 2 feet square rocks with an open 5 gallon bucket! The top word began at approximately 1500 feet—500 yards—(457 meters.) Unbelievable! How great is the grace of God! No wonder I ended up with the words Jesus is coming changed to Jesus Cometh. I was 20 years old and today at 72 I hardly can haul a 5 gallon bucket of water up 7 steps into my boat. What do you expect I am not a chicken anymore!

A good part of the suburb of Primrose being the largest suburb in the world at the time and being built upon a hill looked down upon this sign. Many, many people were to be daily reminded that the coming of our Lord Jesus was imminent.

One day being a passenger in a Boeing airplane which flew over the sign I witnessed American passengers in front of me taking photos of the sign. Of course my embarrassing stutter forbade me to tell them I painted the sign. I heard them exclaiming repeatedly that the city we were flying over was bigger than Chicago.

Whilst I being unemployed and my friends being employed I spent days and weeks painting the sign alone, but I do remember some help from some of my friends, Martin van Wyk, Martin and Henry Boyens, Theo Erasmus and Ashley Campbell. Rejoice guys—there's reward in heaven!

The white wash lasted one year and then the sign had to be repainted. I painted it for three consecutive years and then moved away from the area. That was around 1964. Amazingly the sign was repainted every year. I never did find out by whom but I believe it was a youth group of some local church. The newspaper article appearing below was dated November 10, 1989, so this group painted it at least 25 years.

On another note of humor, my friends and I painted another sign on a mine dump just outside the factory namely 3M-company, where I was employed. The sign read "SIN LEADS TO HELL" sometime later on arriving at work I saw the sign was changed to "GIN LEADS TO HEALTH." Later we again changed it back to the original.

GERMISTON CITY NEWS, FRIDAY, NOVEMBER 10, 1989   PAGE 5

Landmark will go as dump is reclaimed

Germiston will be losing a unique landmark but residents who direct their friends to turn left at the 'Jesus cometh' mine-dump need not rush out and check the street names (Main Reef and Homestead) - it will still be there for another 14 years.

The reclamation of the landmark "Awake Jesus Cometh" mine dump, by Knights Gold Mining Company, is expected to yield R41,9-million annually.

But although the reclamation will be profitable the disap-

pearance of the dump is also a cause for regret - this familiar landmark has been around for over 20 years.

Councillor for the ward, Clr Johann Rossouw, a member of Germiston City Council's management committee, said: "My friends and a group of people from overseas have visited Germiston and have specifically referred to the writing on the mine dump as being a positive message for spiritual revival.

This revival, said Clr Rossouw, took place in the late '60s and a local

Christian group (now disbanded) asked permission to paint the message on the dump.

However, a spokesman for Knights Gold Mining Company said: "It's our mine and nobody has complained or even asked us to repaint the message".

The total capital outlay for the reclamation has been R43-million.

At full capacity the Knights plant is designed to produce 1 396kg of gold annually which, based on a gold price of R30 000 a kilogram, will produce the annual revenue of R41,9 m.

The "Awake Jesus Cometh" landmark mine dump has about 14 years left to proclaim its message.

1. THESSALONIANS, 5:2
For yourselves know perfectly that the day of the Lord so cometh as a thief in the night.

1967

The big crocodile—hearing the voice of God

Back in the early sixties, I was asked to eradicate a very large crocodile which was responsible for the loss of human lives. I inspected the area and was amazed to see the size of the tracks and imprints left on the sand. Upon placing my open hand within the print of its foot, my hand was circumvented with a two inch border. This was truly a large one. I contacted my hunting buddy by the name of Tinus Cronje and invited him to accompany me.

Both with a .375 Holland and Holland Magnum, we set out at night with a powerful spotlight, and I had a little hunting light secured to my forehead. As it was my contact and I being the contacted person to shoot this reptile, I should obviously have done the shooting, whilst Tinus would have held the light in position. For some reason, which I later knew was the leading of God, I requested Tinus to take the shot, whilst I held the light. This was a divinely appointed miracle and most certainly saved a life.

As we approached the river, we soon saw the red glow of the crocodile's eye. This insidious creature was the cause of much grief among the local population.

Not only had we seen it, but it had seen us, gauged our line of walk and had crossed from the opposite side, where we had seen it and lay in wait for us next to a low lying rock which protruded into the water. Miracle no. 2 came when we did not pass the rock, but walked directly onto it. It was lying in wait for us, no more than a foot from the bank. Tinus positioned himself in a sitting position on the frontal edge of the rock, whilst I stood close behind. As the rock was narrow and he being in front, he now held the light and scrutinized the area. Unbeknown to us, the crocodile was now coming up behind us and was already in the throes of the catch.

Miracle no. 3 came next. This was none other than the voice of God and thanks be to Him, I have always been able to hear and discern His voice. This spiritual voice said: "Look right at your feet." I then did something I had never done in the past and under normal circumstances, certainly would never do. This was to shine a light behind the person in front. Not only would this reveal your position to the crocodile, thereby causing danger to yourself, but it would caution the crocodile.

I took the little lamp off my forehead and shone no more than a yard (meter) from us into the water. The crocodile was just about to propel itself onto us, and the light blinded his final move. The river was crystal clear and it was an awesome sight to see the cunning smile as it backtracked under water and repositioned itself for another attack. Tinus reacted in haste and upon getting up in much of a hurry, was about to fall right onto the crocodile. I was fortunate to catch him by his shirt and steady him. The crocodile moved around the rock and being under water obviously thought he was invisible to us. The powerful lamp illuminated this leviathan of the river, pitting hunter against hunter, both in their own acquired way. As the crocodile emerged some four feet from us, Tinus shot, but having a telescope on his rifle, obviously shot low into the jaw, due to close range. This crocodile, having tasted human flesh before on several occasions, now followed us on shore. It was hissing loudly and intent on killing us so I quickly finished it off. It was so heavy that three of us could not even roll it over.

"Now thanks be unto God who doth always cause us to triumph in Christ Jesus." (2 Corinthians 2:14)

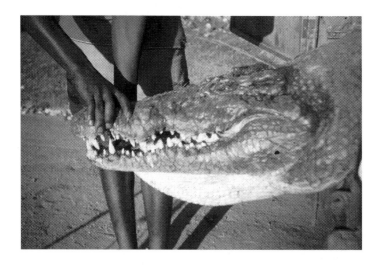

An Enormous Crocodile

The six dolphins

Along the most northeasterly border of South Africa adjoining the southeasterly border of its neighboring country, Mozambique, lays the most shark infested area of the world. This fact I had learned from a TV documentary naming the ten most shark infested areas of the world. The said area was named as number one. Its general area stretched from Sodwana Bay in South Africa northward through Kosi Bay, Malongane and along the coast of the Maputo Elephant Game Reserve.

As any road to these places was in the worst condition possible for travel, only the hardiest of adventurers with a four wheel drive and caravan/trailer would holiday there. I found this place to be the lost paradise of scuba diving and spear fishing. Its coral reefs stand second to none other when it comes to the gorgeous display of color. This fantastic Zululand coast proved to be the paradise lost of many adventures for me. One such experience I will name as the "Miracle of the six dolphins."

Our normal scuba diving excursions took us far out beyond breakwater. It required a ferocious swim through thundering waves. As from a boy I have always been blessed as a strong swimmer and it was always an awesome experience to dive deep under these rolling torrents of water and watch them from beneath. As these thunderous waves were the cause of many overturned sportsman's boats, it required only the strongest of swimmers to break surf and get "behind water." Once there, however, one could enjoy the bluest, clearest waters and abundance of marine life that Planet Earth could offer. Upon reaching the colorful coral reefs, one was entreated to a display of coral fish, bottom fish, barracuda and sharks of many species. Manta and electric rays, turtles, etc. were always in abundance.

On this day, however, as named, the day of the Miracle of the Six Dolphins, I was well within breakwater, being no more than 150 meters/yards from shore. I was suddenly surrounded by six dolphins. It was an awesome sight. They were so near that I tried to touch them and came as near as six inches from them. Around and around they encircled me, with their smiling faces. I was so taken up with this spectacular sight that I called to my good friend, Yan Venter to come and see. He obviously saw my excitement and quickly swam to me, only to find me encircled by what he then thought were sharks. He soon learned, however, that this was not a visit of peril but rather of protection.

During the course of being closely encircled by these beautiful animals/mammals, five would suddenly leave, whilst one still remained. The five would soon return, continue to encircle us and then suddenly speed off again, leaving one with us. This strange but friendly gesture continued four of five times, and then they suddenly all left, leaving us feeling blessed and thankful for a God given visit by some of His greatest creatures.

The true blessing, however, came a few hours later when another friend by the name of Alf Jones came to tell me that a shark had just washed ashore, that had been killed by dolphins.

Well do I recall a newspaper article which I once read, wherein a young lady described her experience of a similar nature. She related how that she, with two male partners, had been fishing near the coast of the Island of Inhaca. Their boat had overturned, resulting in the drowning of her two friends. She, being a strong swimmer, decided to swim some twenty five miles back to Lorenzo Marques, now renamed as Maputo, the capital city of Mozambique.

During the course of her long swim, she suddenly found herself surrounded by sharks, and being an atheist, she called out and said, "God, if you are real, please reveal yourself to me at this time of certain death." Within seconds, dolphins came to her rescue. They dispersed the sharks and accompanied her on her long swim back to shore. Along the way they helped her climb on a shipping buoy, where a ship finally rescued her. I cherished that story, and more than once, preached about it and the great loving God who heard the heart-wrenching call of an atheist in dire distress. Above all, I loved her remark, "Now I know there is a God in Heaven!" Glory be to His Name!

"If it had not been the Lord that was on our side, then the waters had overwhelmed us, the stream had gone over our soul. Our soul is escaped as a bird out of the snare of the fowlers: the snare is broken, and we are escaped. Our help is in the Name of the Lord, who made heaven and earth." (Psalms 124: 2, 4, 7 and 8)

"I waited patiently for the Lord; and he inclined unto me, and heard my cry. He brought me up also out of a horrible pit, out of the miry clay, and set my feet upon a rock, and established my goings. And he hath put a new song in my mouth, even praise unto our God: many shall see it, and fear, and shall trust the Lord." (Psalms 40:1-3)

In peril of drowning

At age twenty six I designed and built my own aluminum spear gun which I still have today, forty seven years later. During the years, I really treasured this spear gun.

During one of our spear fishing episodes at Sodwana Bay we teamed up with a stranger who mentioned that he was a school teacher. During our entry into the colossal surf he got into trouble and very reluctantly I dropped my spear gun to help him and was glad that I could be instrumental in helping save his life. I fortunately found the spear gun again and continued my spear fishing. I shot a beautiful Parrot fish and could already see it mounted and hanging on my wall.

A problem arose however, as the fish was in a cave and the arrow/ spear was hooked. I had enough line on the reel to reach the surface and was now battered by immense waves jettisoning me against terrible rocks. I considered casting my gun away but somehow did not give it a second thought. I decided live or die, I would not lose my gun, but the more I fought to save it, the more I got entwined in the string and was now very near to drowning. Again God must have sent one of his angels with a command like: "Go and help that one who cares more for his gun than his life!" Suddenly the spear and fish came loose and I was rolled out over the rocks, badly cut, bruised and injured. Below is a picture of the mounted Parrot fish and spear gun.

With my home built 47 year old spear gun

The mounted Fish that nearly cost me my life.

The big Shark

Talking of my good friend, Yan Venter, I do recall Yan's initiation to spear fishing. If my memory serves me well, it was the day before the Miracle of the Dolphins. I invited Yan to accompany me to the backwaters. He gladly accepted, and while breaking through the surf, I had a glimpse of a tremendously huge shark. The image of its awesome agility still remains with me today and is forever burnt into my memory. It was clearly "on the prey," for with one flick of its tail; it would propel itself with immense speed, and then suddenly turn and change direction. I was awestruck at this tremendous sight, but very nervous when my vision was restricted in foaming water.

Many species of man-eating sharks inhabit these waters and whether it was the same shark or another I do not know. What I do know is that I had speared some five fish of a good and envious size, and secured them to a rope which in turn was secured to my weight belt no more than six feet away. Whilst I had speared the latest fish and was in the throes of pulling its gills apart to ensure a hasty death, which obviously resulted in much erratic movement and blood from the fish, I became abruptly aware of the danger of the moment. The panic-stricken movement and blood of the fish was a sure shark attraction. I looked up to see if there was any impending danger and looked straight into the opening jaws of a very rapidly moving, very large shark no more than three feet from me. Instinctively, I yanked the fish away from the gaping jaws which revealed a barrage of rows of razor-like teeth. It was evident the shark wanted my fish. The only problem was that I was very reluctant to forfeit my hard earned delicious catch.

What ensued in the next five to ten minutes was a continual attack by a twelve feet shark coming for my bunch of fish. I would hold them at arm's length and as the shark's mouth opened, I would yank them away. This necessitated a repeated attack by the shark. During all this time Yan was screaming and pulling on me. At one time, I heard him say, *"Pastor, are you mad?"* And this remark probably saved my life. As sanity dawned upon me, I cut the line and with much remorse gave up my five stump-nose fish, each weighing approximately seven pounds.

Later, Yan explained more fully the reason for his excited shouting. He said that at one stage, the shark was coming from behind, had actually turned onto its side, positioned itself for attack and for some unknown reason, whether by lift of wave or whatever, shot past under me.

The other reason for shouting was for me to employ the "thunderhead" onto my spear and thereby shoot the shark. This device is a twelve bore shotgun which is positioned on the tip of the spear, and when shot at the shark, detonates upon impact. I was so sidetracked by the saving of my fish that it never occurred to me what an impact it would have had upon all to have had a boat come and pull a twelve to fifteen foot shark on shore.

Perhaps it was for the good of all. I doubt if any of the holiday makers would have again entered the water. I still feel remorse for having missed the opportunity of posing for a photo with a most notable trophy, but on the other hand, I feel pleased that a fair bargain was struck. The shark saved my life and I in turn, saved his.

May I state that I met many species of sharks on many occasions, and never once did any ever reveal any personal vindictiveness? If this was God's protection or just the natural nature of the shark, I do not know, but what I do know is that when I viewed the showing of that absurd far-fetched movie, Jaws, I was immensely infuriated. It portrayed a false nature of the shark and no doubt resulted in unnecessary paranoia of fear amongst holiday makers and an unnecessary slaughter of these wonderful carrion cleaners of the seas.

I am told that many species of so called man eating sharks inhabit these waters, like the Mako, Blue Pointer, Zambezi/Bull, Hammerhead, Tiger, etc. I believe it was my privilege to have seen most of them. I am however, very thankful that I have never had the ill-fated misfortune of confrontation with the "Great White." Suffice it to say that it is enough to watch the many tourist vessels leaving right in front of a house owned by my family at Van Dyksbaai (Kleinbaai), Cape, to view the Great Whites. These films have repeatedly been shown on Discovery Network. The Great Whites' domicile is in the cold western Augulas current of the Atlantic Ocean, where my escapades all took place in the warm eastern Indian Ocean.

I often am awestruck by the grace given to my friend, Yan Venter. His life has always been from one extreme to the other. Well do I recall his "baptism by fire" into the experiences of diving on the Zululand coast! I believe it was his first three days of initiation into diving that the dolphin experience, the big shark experience and the following occurred. Yan and I broke surf and swam with vehemence into deeper water. We had to swiftly distance ourselves from the current of the waves. I was in front, Yan shortly behind at my feet on the left side, when I heard his muffled calls in his mask. On looking back, I saw a pair of eyes as wide as saucers. The source of concern was an immense tiger shark that had joined our formation, and was swimming shortly behind Yan, at his feet. My first impression was that the shark meant no harm. This impression was definitely not shared by Yan. The occasion caused me to break into uncontrollable fits of laughter. This occurrence is not easily practiced within a face mask. It necessitates the removal of the mask and to end your laughing streak above water whilst a "man-eating predator" is no more than six feet away. With me positioned in front, Yan between me and the shark, this was a similarity to the joke wherein two guys were confronted by a bear. Said the one to the other, "Don't run; you can't outrun a bear!" Said the other in response, "I don't need to outrun the bear; I only need to outrun you!" Yan later explained that his source of concern was not fear, but to gain my attention to the shark and perhaps use the thunderhead. He also explained that whist I was laughing he dived toward the shark and so scared it away.

The following chapter I have extracted verbatim from Yan Venter's book *"You won't believe this"* I had forgotten about this experience so when Yan wrote it, it was a reminder to me.

Hunting a Croc

"Croc" hunting was something I had never done until I met John Hitchcock. Crocodiles, unlike most alligators are dangerous creatures. You are never safe when you set your foot into croc-infested waters. They are "beasts" in the water that will go after anything and anyone. They are extremely cunning hunters, able to creep up and surprise their prey without ever being seen. I have watched a croc surprise and attack an antelope that was standing alert. The croc moves silently forward until he is only inches from the snout of an animal drinking at a water hole. Then, with lightning speed he makes his move, dragging the unsuspecting animal into the water and to its death! Yes, crocodiles are arguably some of the craftiest hunters in the animal kingdom. They are definitely not to be messed with! The safest place around a crocodile is on dry land or inside a boat. Even then, you must keep your eyes open and watch! They are certainly not the kind of animal I like to tangle with, that's for sure!

Just before church service one night, John approached me with the news that we had an invitation to hunt some crocs on a nearby farmer's land. He explained that the farmer was having a problem with three crocs that had moved into his pond and had been responsible for attacking his livestock. He wanted them shot and approached John asking him to do it. The farmer explained that two of the crocs were rather small, but the third one was a "monster." Hunting crocs is best done at night with a spotlight. Their eyes reflect "blood red" in the light making them easy to spot.

"Ol' Buddy," John enthusiastically approached. "This is a rare opportunity for us and I want you in on the hunt." Without even thinking twice I said "yes" and asked him when we would be going. "We'll go straight after church tonight. The crocs should be out in the water when we get there."

I could hardly wait for the service to be over! My heart was filled with so much excitement! I knew John was an experienced croc hunter and this would be an opportunity for me to learn from him. After being his friend for many years, I have learned to be doubly careful around John because of his many crazy stunts, but for some reason, this time I wasn't.

After the service, we went over to his house to get the gear ready. We picked up a battery for the searchlights—one for each of us. But when we tested them, only one was in working condition. So John said, "We really don't need two. One will suffice."

We gathered a long rope with a grapple at the end. The grapple had three hooks. John explained to me that this would be used to get the croc up after it was shot, as the croc is very valuable for its skin. Then he picked up two of his rifles. The .22 rifle would be used on the small crocs, and the .375 Magnum, would be used on the big one. His "garden boy" would go along with us to carry the heavy car battery. Then we started off to the farmer's pond on my first croc-hunting expedition.

I was so excited! This was a "first" for me and I could not wait to learn from John. Somewhere inside me though, was a small nagging feeling, because, as I said before, I didn't feel very safe around this "adventure-crazed" friend of mine. Though I am the adventuresome type and always ready for a challenge, John thrived in danger. It even seemed, at times, if there were no danger in a situation, he would create some.

Late that night we arrived on the farm and headed straight for the "pond." As we got closer I noticed that it was more than a pond. It was really a small lake with light fog hovering over the water. We moved very quietly to avoid "spooking" the crocs. Very discreetly, we unloaded the gear. I picked up the rope and hung it around one shoulder, then the .375 Magnum which I hung around my other shoulder, John held the light in one hand and the .22 in the other.

"Where's the boat?" I asked, somewhat surprised, as we headed toward the waterfront. "No, there's no boat, but we won't need one," John told me. "We'll do it all by foot."

He explained that we would walk around the lake in the water, to avoid making noise. When I protested, he explained, "There's no problem Buddy, we'll be able to see the eye well before there are problems!"

I didn't feel very safe, "But then," I reasoned, "he knows better. He's the Croc hunter."

It took a lot of persuasion to get the "garden boy" to follow us into the water, but eventually he did, and when I looked back, I could clearly see the whites of his eyes! His face was filled with fear and I knew that it wouldn't take much for him to make a dash for dry land if the slightest problem should occur.

We moved into the water until we were knee-deep, circling the lake with caution as John continued to sweep the light, left to right, looking for the "red eye." The air was filled with the sounds of huge bullfrogs croaking out their "groggy" songs. Crickets were filling in the gaps when the frog's voices were not heard. Tonight there was no moon. It was a dark night, ideal for the searchlight to show any sign of movement. The fog was hanging lightly over the water, creating an even more sinister atmosphere. This situation was dangerous and I could feel it.

We had circled more than half the lake when suddenly we spotted the first red eye. It was about fifty feet from the shore. John carefully inspected the eye that was reflected in the light, then whispered, "It's one of the small ones. Step out to the side and leave the .375 on the bank. You will need both your hands to fling the rope after I've shot it. Then you will have to hold the light and shine it over my shoulder so that I can take the shot."

Hesitantly, I walked the few yards back to dry land, laid the big gun on the grass and joined John and the "garden boy." Carefully, we moved deeper toward the red eye. "This is crazy" I told myself. I'm not worried about the one we can see, but the one we cannot see, because John is holding the light fixed on the eye in front of us. We were moving deeper and deeper into the water, until it was almost up to my elbows.

The eyes of the croc sat close together, which told us that it was the small one, but when we got within 15 feet of him, he turned toward us and we realized it WASN'T the small one! He was positioned halfway away from us, but looking directly at us. John whispered, "Ol' Buddy, it's the BIG ONE!"

Carefully he took aim while I held the spotlight over his shoulder and the barrel of the gun. When the shot rang out, the croc went down. Without being careful about making noises now, I spoke out loudly and asked him "What now?" The croc was no longer visible, and where he went under the water, small circles appeared on the surface.

"I think I got him," John informed me.

"What do you mean, you think . . . ?" It wasn't enough for me to hear him say, "I think." We're almost up to our necks in water and he's not sure!

"Well, what now?" I asked the croc hunter.

"Let's start looking for him." I saw John walk around the spot, searching for the "dead" croc with his feet.

I could hear the garden boy making disgruntled noises. His face had an expression of total fear and unbelief, but as yet he was with us, still holding onto the car battery. Reluctantly, I joined in the search with my feet, trying to feel where the dead croc was supposed to be. Nervously, I moved the light all around to see if I could see any sign of him, knowing that if he was alive, he would not show up on the surface, but would, instead go for one of our legs.

"Ol' Buddy," John said, "I don't think I got him!"

When I asked, "What now?" he firmly suggested we get out of the water as fast as possible! That's all that the garden boy needed to hear, and without any concern for the light, or us he made his move out of the water. With the battery still on his shoulder while making his escape, the light was yanked completely out of my hand. Due to this sudden turn of events, I was not far behind him and John was right behind me, laughing as he came.

I have never appreciated dry land as much as when I made my way out of the water that night. I threw the grapple hook and rope down with disgust. The garden boy had moved a few more yards further up the slope to make sure that he was VERY safe! John took the light and shone it over the water, and right there behind us; the big croc made his appearance for a split second, and then disappeared never to be seen by us again.

That was the end of our croc hunting experience. There was no way the garden boy would go into the water again, and to tell the truth, neither would I! I love my friend John, but I would not hunt crocs again until years later, when I did it on my own terms!

Zebras provide water in a barren land

Typical of myself, who never plans but rushes headlong, because of haste, anxiousness and excitement, I left on a day's hunting trip. It was near Mica/Hoedspruit, east of the Drakensburg and it was a hot blistering day, as only one who knows the hot "bushveld" of South Africa, can appreciate.

Shamefacedly I admit that I began a day's hunt with no canteen of water or food. I never was one to hunt from a vehicle but always preferred walking and many days would see me cover 20-30 miles. By midday I was really suffering due to thirst. All excitement about hunting was now superseded by a need for water, so I prayed for water! I was walking next to a dry river bed that had obviously not seen water for many months, and passing a heap of river sand in the middle of the riverbed, I wondered if there was any hope of finding water. The idea seemed ridiculous and impossible and I continued to walk away. Then a thought came to me and I asked myself. John, what type of expectancy and faith have you? Did you not ask God for water? So I turned around and headed back to the heap of sand.

Arriving there amidst tracks of zebra and wildebeest, I found a one yard/meter deep hole dug out by the Zebras at the bottom of which was the coolest, clearest water. When one is as thirsty as I was, a plan will definitely be invented to get your head down a one yard hole, and quench your thirst. I did.

"Then shall the lame man leap as a hart, and the tongue of the dumb sing: for in the wilderness shall waters break out, and streams in the desert." Isaiah 35:6

Thank you Jesus!

A joke backfires

The priority of many people visiting national parks in Africa is the captivating sight of the "big five." Whilst I do not deny this, I really do find a lot of joy watching baboons! With them, there is always something going on. Humor is abundant and laughter continues. As God created baboons, He certainly does have a sense of humor. It was on one of these days that I was stealthily strolling near the junction of the Selati and Olifants rivers when I came suddenly and unexpectedly on a troop of baboons who scattered, amidst a roar of screams and barks in various directions. As a point of interest, have you dear reader, ever thought what is the sign God gave to man when He said:

". . . and let them have dominion over the fish of the sea and over the fowl of the air, and over the cattle, and over all the earth, and over every creeping thing that creepeth upon the earth." (Gen 1:26)

I submit to you it is the "homo-erectus" sign. Man walks upright and that is the sign the animals fear, respect and acknowledge. (I once crawled up to four lions and they just watched me and when I stood up, they scattered in all directions.) Let us assume for a moment that prehistoric man lived amongst Dinosaurs. It must have been terrible fear to be subject to the authority of animals.

Back to the story of the baboons, after they scattered, one was trapped above me in a giant old Sycamore tree, and I decided to have some fun. Circling under the tree I pretended to aim the rifle at him every time I got a glimpse of him. How that big old baboon managed to conceal himself behind a thin branch, I will never comprehend. Every now and then an eye peeped around the side of the branch and then quickly retracted again. However, it had now become clear to the baboon that I knew his whereabouts and that another plan had to be officiated.

Well, that's exactly what happened. Next thing, an arm was hurled around the branch and lumps of excreta (crap) caught me full in the face. The assault continued more than once. So without further ado, I conceded defeat and laughingly walked away. My joke had backfired and I was the loser.

Sodwana Bay—Zululand

I've always loved the wild places. Cruises, grand hotels and luxury have never appealed to me. The wilderness, including danger has always reigned supreme in my adventurous spirit. Where most people would vacation in the high condos of Durban, I much preferred camping in a tent in the wilds.

Nevertheless I had just purchased a brand new travel trailer (caravan) for evangelism and was very proud of my new "mobile home." It was vacation time and I decided to take the caravan to Sodwana Bay in Zululand. So having hitched her behind my four wheel drive, newly painted Jeep Cherokee, I took the long road from Johannesburg, to the turn off from the asphalt road of the exit to Sodwana Bay. This extremely primitive, rough, potholed, sand road, necessitated some 60 miles of sand road. En route, I was confronted with a fork in the road. There was no sign of direction to Sodwana, so I had to guess. Obviously I decided on the one which looked the most traveled, and so the bumpy miles continued one after the other. The problem was that the road became narrower and narrower. Finally it became no more than a cattle track. Thorn Acacia trees was abundant and very soon both newly painted Jeep and new Caravan was subjected to squeezing and scratching between the trees. To say the least it was heart breaking. There was no place for turn around and too many miles were now passed. From my former crocodile hunting days, I knew there was a road leading from the south to Sodwana. I had previously traveled it and so I just set my mind to reach it. By now I had to engage four wheel drive and drag the vehicles through the scraping thorns. It was heartrending! Judging the distance, I knew I had to be near the road now but great consternation overwhelmed me when I came on the banks of a swamp/ come river. Due to crocodiles, I certainly would not wade through it to fathom its depth. Turning around was an impossibility and backtracking those miles was not even a consideration, so without further hesitation, I engaged second gear and with full acceleration I plunged into the river.

God be thanked again as I just kept going and finally scaled the opposite bank. A few miles further I came upon the road to Sodwana, and arrived safely there some time later. Truly,

"The angel of the Lord encampeth round about them that fear him, and delivereth them." (Psalms 34:7)

Viva—the professional hunter

Many of you reading this book will experience the proverbial "raised eyebrows" about my hunting experiences. Many believe that hunting a poor animal is a grievous "no-no," but in fact it is the hunter that is a real animal lover and by reading through this book you will notice that apart from God and this work, my love of paramount importance is a love of animals, birds and nature.

I have been the proud pet owner of many wild animals' viz. monkey, hawks, owl, crow, mongoose, eagles, crocodile, etc.

Strangely, those who condemn hunting are the ones who eat meat, wear leather shoes, and so on. The greatest threat to wildlife has been none other than the cow. When the cattle and sheep farmers came, wild animals had to go. Carnivorous animals had to be exterminated and all other game would encroach on grazing fodder. Their presence was not desirable.

South Africa, the land of my birth is a good example. In all the years I lived there, game had been exterminated in order to make room for the farmer. The only wild animals were sheltered in game reserves. Very few were found on farms. Then a great revolution occurred, lets' call it "THE ERA OF THE PROFFESIONAL HUNTER." Farmers began to discover that there was much more money to be made in breeding game, and invite overseas hunters to a safari. The price of hunting game became far more lucrative than farming with crops or cattle and sheep. Game farming hit the exponential curve. Farmers began to build lodges, plant indigenous trees and breed with game. On my recent visit to South Africa I was astonished to find an overwhelming interest in wild animals. It was found that the professional hunter would come and pay an exorbitant price to only pull a trigger. The farmer would keep the meat, hides, taxidermy profit etc., whilst the hunter possessed only the thrill of experiencing an African Safari and a mounted trophy to remind him of his joy. I personally have friends who have sold and relinquished their businesses and opened safari lodges. South Africa now has more game than since its occupation by Europeans.

Auctions of stock have been rivaled by auctions of game. When I was back in January 2012, I witnessed a "golden Wildebeest" which was being bred which sells for more than a million Rand. The big cats are being sold for millions of Rand. Where once they were near to extinction they have now made a superb comeback.

So dear friend, please do not judge me for my hunting experiences but read between the lines and discover my great love of wild animals. A true hunter is a true animal conserver. Thank God for the professional hunter!

MORE EXPERIENCES WITH TINUS CRONJE

A black night of danger on the Olifants River

In 1967 a cousin of mine by way of marriage named Hendrik visited us in Phalaborwa. He had heard that we occasionally hunted crocodiles and expressed an interest to accompany us. I arranged with Pastor Cronje. Our plan was to load our little 8ft metal dingy (nothing more than a bathtub) onto the roof of my Land Rover. We would leave his Volvo way down stream, then continue upstream, load the boat into the river and sail downstream. We had no motor but had a pair of oars.

Plans accomplished, we launched the boat on a dark moonless night and proceeded to drift down the river. By this time Hendrik, a city boy was already expressing concerns about the safety and intelligence of this trip. We had been talking about the danger of hippos. More people in Africa are killed by hippos than any other animal. Apart from the glowing red eyes of crocodiles which we could not reach by rowing due to the current being too strong, we saw the gleam of some fifteen to twenty hippos downstream from us. Hendrik now began giving strict orders to beach this bathtub and get the h . . l out of here. Again the paddling did not work and all too soon we were in the middle of the hippos—all snorting and blowing, heads emerging and submerging one yard from us. Hendrik hit panic stations.

We passed over the pod without incident whereas it would have been the easiest thing for some sport loving calf to capsize us and make us crocodile bait. From water level to top side (gun rails) of our bathtub would be 4 inches.

Next we heard the sound of a waterfall ahead, and being now caught in rapids we thrust the oar into the rocks to block the swift flow of the boat. The oar snapped like a match. As we continued floating down stream, we approached the waterfall. Hendrik was not a happy camper and began swearing at the pastor and myself informing us in no uncertain terms that he was a married father with children and this was very irresponsible. How could we venture down an uncharted, unknown river and that on a dark night? Being opportunistic adventurers, we obviously had no answer. We tried steering with the one oar but having no keel, it was to no avail. The thunderous roar of the waterfall was now near and we were at our wits end. Thank God the angels kicked into gear and helped bathtub fall between rocks, some 10ft from the waterfall's edge. Fortunately we were not too far from the bank, some 45 foot. We then took the grapple iron (being a big 3 clawed hook with a rope attached to it) and began throwing it over the branches of the trees being ever so careful not to buck the boat and thereby plunge us over the waterfall. With the three of us tugging on the gripped rope we managed to reach shore. Now we had to carry bathtub thru waist deep water to the bottom of the waterfall. Having reached our destination we abandoned the venture and sailed further to the waiting car without incident. When we arrived home Hendrik immediately fell into the arms of his wife and fell asleep.

Saved from a charging buffalo

One other incident with Pastor Tinus Cronje warrants mentioning. We had traveled to Mozambique where my uncle had a farm on the Revue River between Umtali and Tete. It was rife with big game. Whilst out hunting we met a young Portuguese guy and he joined our party. He had a light caliber rifle but Tinus and I had the .375 magnum—a good buffalo rifle. We came across a buffalo and both Tinus and the Portuguese guy fired and landed badly placed shots into her. We now had a wounded Cape buffalo on our hands. A wounded buffalo is the most dangerous of African game. Whilst tracking its spoor, I was some 25 yards on the right and happened to see a large high anthill. I climbed up and saw the buffalo hiding in a thicket at the edge of an open space. In an instant Tinus ventured into the area and he was about midway when the buffalo charged. Tinus's nerves gave in and he bolted for the nearest tree taking refuge behind it. As the buffalo came around the tree for the kill I was able to place a shot in the neck and it fell at Tinus's feet. The front cover page chronicles this buffalo and the tree where Tinus stood is immediately to the left but just out of the picture.

He said his rifle jammed, and if so he would surely have been killed.

1968

I fight a ghost

During my stay in Phalaborwa, South Africa, I worked at both Phalaborwa Mining Company and later at Foskor. I do believe these are two major copper mines in the world. My duties included working as a laboratory sampler in the concentrator. With periodic visits to the laboratory to test the samples of copper content and Titanium, I heard the samplers and laboratory technicians talking about the ghost in the laboratory. I did not give much attention to the subject until one night whilst on night shift (graveyard shift) my church associate and co-worker asked me to pray for him. I queried the reason and he stated that he is petrified to perform his duties in the laboratory because of an evil presence which haunts the place. I responded "you know Alan, I have heard the guys talk about this, please explain the situation." So we walked next door to the laboratory and walking down a brightly lit, white painted passage, similar to a hospital we were suddenly encompassed by a terrible evil presence. All my hair stood on edge and I noticed his beard looked like trembling prickly pears (cactus needles.) My first thought was that it was some presence from the morgue (mortuary) which was attached to the end of the laboratory and divided by only a wall. This fight seemed right "up my alley" as I had already grown spiritually and knew my authority in Christ. I knew Alan was still a "babe in Christ" so I suggested that he return to his duties whilst I remained and rectified this situation.

The presence was exceedingly evil and terrifying but I knew I was safe under the blood of Jesus so in great disrespect to the devil (like David to Goliath) I challenged him on his own grounds. I put off all the lights, shut myself in a stark pitch dark room and confronted the demon/spirit in the Name of Jesus. It retaliated with extreme force of such viciousness that I was actually aware that if I was not protected by the blood and power of Christ, my physical life would be in jeopardy. I began to bind and rebuke this spirit. It was a vicious combat and after some time, I believed I had gained the victory. Perhaps some haste to retreat from the uncomfortable atmosphere persuaded my decision. After switching on the lights I proceeded to evacuate the laboratory but before the exit, I was made aware that the situation had not been finalized so I initiated the experience again, lights put off and enclosed myself in the dark room.

After another intense battle in the Name of Jesus I commanded the demonic spirit to leave and never return. I had formerly learned that when we fight the devil we should gain complete victory, not half measures. Suddenly, I felt victory within my spirit and a great peace descended upon my mind, soul and spirit. I returned to Alan and shared the news.

Later I heard the guys talking about the ghost that was no longer there, but like Mary of old, whether it was that I knew they would not understand or again fear to talk because of my stutter, I just "hid it in my heart."

To further illustrate the "believers authority" I include hereunder a chapter in my book called the "Gifts of Healing"—written 40 years ago. Capitalization remains the same as at that time.

The believers' authority

Authority carries a strange magic. The idle employee hastily busies himself when the foreman or boss is near. A dart of fear constantly pierces the heart of a criminal when a policeman is near: and every devil trembles in the presence of an anointed child of God. But will the idle employee react, if his boss does not know how to enforce his authority? So the devil will resist his defeat, if the child of God does not know what his rights and authority are in the name of Jesus.

When Jesus arose from the dead, He left Satan behind Him, ETERNALLY DEFEATED!

Colossians 2:15 states "Having spoiled principalities and powers He (Jesus) made a show of them openly, triumphing over them in it."

"Wherefore God also hath highly exalted Him, and given Him a name that is above every name, that at the Name of Jesus every knee

should bow, of things in heaven (angels) and things in earth (men) and things under the earth (devils and demons.)" (Philippians 2:9-10)

Thus we see that Jesus holds full sway over the forces of darkness. Every devil fears and trembles at the name of Jesus. *Luke 8:30, 31; James 2:19.* Jesus means what He says, and says what He means.

"All power is given unto me in heaven and in earth." (Matt 28:18)

I want you now to notice very carefully, because YOU are involved in this. Jesus did not conquer the devil for himself. He always had been the conqueror, but He entered human flesh *(John 1:14; Phil 2: 7, 8)* and conquered the devil in HUMAN FLESH. This is of great significance, for if Jesus conquered Satan in HUMAN FLESH then JESUS could give His victory UNTO HUMAN FLESH, and this is just what He did.

Note carefully, *God has set Jesus Christ at His own right hand in the HEAVENLY places (realms of power and authority) FAR ABOVE ALL principality, and power and might and every name that is named . . . and hath put ALL things under His feet and gave Him to be the head over all things to the Church. (Ephesians 1:20-21)* Christ is seated in HEAVENLY PLACES of power and authority.

But where do you and I get involved? LISTEN, PERCEIVE AND UNDERSTAND! *Ephesians 2:6* states God has RAISED US UP TOGETHER IN HEAVENLY PLACES IN CHRIST JESUS! Hallelujah!

Christ's authority over demons, sickness and disease is our authority of demons, sickness and disease. Christ's power over SATAN IS OUR power over Satan. You needn't fast and pray for power over the devil. You HAVE power over him. We are JOINT-HEIRS with Christ! *Romans 8:17.* Jesus prays to His Father saying:

"The glory Thou gavest me, I have given unto them, that they may be one, even as we are one, I in them, and Thou in me, that they may be made perfect in one." (John 17:22, 23)

"And YE are complete in Him, which is the head of all principality and power." (Col. 2:10)

Precious friend, why do you fear sickness, disease and infirmity, why do you fear the devil, why do you fear? "Behold" said Jesus

"I give unto you, power over all the power of the enemy, and NOTHING shall by any means hurt you." (Luke 10:19)

Now that you KNOW your power of attorney, start using it! You will stand amazed as you see every sickness and work of the devil flee before your face. You have the right to command in Jesus name for YOU are an *"ambassador"* for Christ Jesus. (*2 Cor. 5:20*)

I, as a stammerer am given the authority to take dominion over my stammer, I rebuke it in Jesus' Name and lo and behold, every time I preach, there is no stammer, but I enjoy the liberty through the power of the Spirit. You can do the same. Rebuke your infirmity in the Name of Jesus then act your faith by doing what you could not do before. Confess your victory, saying "I can do all things through Christ which strengthened me." Certainly do not say "Oh I am so sick." For in so doing you are making a negative confession and in so doing you are exalting the devil. Take dominion over him, cast him out, and destroy his works. Christ has appointed YOU unto this. KNOW your rights and use your CALVARY bought authority!

You might, however, not understand how one can rebuke a fever or a cancer or deafness or some form of sickness. Are these then not "deaf" manifestations? How can they then hear and obey a command? I believe this is an intelligent question, but I believe also that the answer is as intelligent. Medical Science is of the opinion that a germ is the cause of infirmity. What Medical Science terms a "germ" God's word terms a "spirit," "demon" or "devil." This "spirit" is a personality. When you therefore rebuke a cancer, you are rebuking the personality behind it, and he is forced to obey.

The Bible says *"for as the body without the spirit is dead . . ."* (*James 2:26*) so having cast out the spirit of cancer, deafness, fever, etc., the body instantly dies. Now the life-giving power of the Spirit touches the dead ear nerves, eye nerves, etc., and instantly the deaf ear hears, and the blind eye sees. Can you see friend, Jesus knew what He was doing when He went about rebuking fig trees and fevers.

Here is a similar exposition given by the Rev. William Branham many years ago: "Every disease has a life—a germ which causes it to function. That evil life in the germ did not come from God, because it kills and destroys human life. It is from Satan. It is that evil life or "spirit of infirmity" that gives life to the disease, or growth, just as your spirit gives life to your body, when the spirit leaves it dies. (*James 2:26*) and returns to the dust, so your disease, when "the spirit of infirmity" is cast out, dies and disappears. We all grew from a tiny germ. The life of that germ came from God. The body, living by the germ or spirit of life which God caused to exist grew and developed until it became a complete human body.

So long as that life or spirit remains in the body, the body continues to live. But as soon as the spirit leaves the body, the body is dead, it decays and returns to the dust. Ever so many afflictions begin from a tiny germ, an evil life, sent to live in and possess the human body and destroy it through some terrible disease. As long as the life or "spirit of infirmity" lives in the body the growth or disease lives on and continues its destructive work. As soon as the evil spirit of "infirmity" has been cast out of the body in Jesus Name, that disease or growth becomes dead. It will decay and pass from the body. This is the process of a HEALING. The life of the disease or growth is rebuked and cast out, and then the effects of the disease or growth pass away in a short time.

When one is healed by a miracle, of course the complete work is instantly wrought by the power of God.

For example, a cancer is a living thing. Its life is satanic. Doctors all agree that if some means could be devised to kill the cancer; to expel the life from the cancer that the effects of that cancer would disappear from the body. But there are two lives warring against each other. The life of the cancer the life which is in your body. And as the present time, any medical means applied to destroy the life of the cancer must be of such force as to also greatly injure, if not destroy the LIFE OF THE BODY, in which the cancer lives.

What is the answer? ONLY FAITH IN THE SUPER-NATURAL POWER AND AUTHORITY OF GOD. According to the Scriptures, Jesus said,

"In my name shall ye cast out devils." In the name of JESUS CHRIST we, as Christians, have the right and authority to expel the spirit or life of the cancer. It is Satanic. When the spirit or life of the cancer, which is from Satan, has departed, the cancer is dead and the effects disappear."

Yes this is the great difference between Divine Healing and Medical Science. Where Divine Healing deals directly with the source or root of the trouble, Medical Science treats the branches and leaves. When you have destroyed the root, the tree dies immediately—but you cut out the leaf of cancer in the human body and it just reveals itself in another place. Why not rather cast out the spirit of cancer and have perfect liberty?

I like the illustration my nephew Evangelist Joel Hitchcock used, and I quote from his book

"Manifesting Christ in You—Identification with the Son of God"

"One day I spent the weekend with my family in Naboomspruit, which was only about 2 1/2 hours away from Pretoria. This time I stayed till Sunday night, and left home around 4 Am., so that I could be at my "point," where I would do my point duty, directing traffic in the city. But yet again, the vehicle, which I affectionately called my *faith-car*, *did* not make it all the way to Pretoria. It always had some mechanical problem. Either the alternator broke, or the carburetor did something, or something happened that broke me down next to the road again. I had two problems: I had to get to College, and before that I had to get to my traffic point. If I did not make it, there would be chaos.

After a while I thought of a very good plan. I put on my traffic cap that looked much like a police hat, my bright orange jacket with the bright yellow line across it, and put on my white gloves. I got right onto the highway and stopped the vehicle of the first poor soul I picked. The driver happened to be a dear older African with a really beat up car. I explained to him what happened. His tense countenance turned into a relieved smile. He told me that he would do anything for me because he was so thankful that I didn't stop him to give him a ticket. Kindly he dropped me at my point. Together we saved Pretoria that day :-)

What made him stop? Was it my little white glove? No, it was the authority it represented. Although I was just a worker for the city, the delegated authority that I possessed made the vehicle stop. Big huge 18-wheeler trucks would obey my hand, covered by the white glove and stop dead in their tracks. There was an authority, a delegated authority that made them obey.

Technically, if they did not obey me, the traffic department could come after them with police helicopters, army tanks and heavy artillery! Of course it wouldn't have gone that far, but the point I am making is that there was a lot of power behind that little white glove.

This is allegorical of the power of the Name of Jesus. Whenever we use the Name of Jesus, we stand in the stead of Jesus, in the shoes of Jesus. It is as if Jesus is in actual operation. In fact, Jesus is indeed in operation! Vested into the Name of Jesus is all the power of God in both heaven and earth. When His Name is mentioned, terror strikes the forces of darkness and every devil and every demon has to bow their knee.

"That <u>at the name of Jesus every knee should bow,</u> of things in heaven, and things in earth, and things under the earth; And that every tongue should confess that Jesus Christ is Lord, to the glory of God the Father." (Philippians 2:10-11, KJV)

1970

Blood poisoning

I was returning from a hunting trip in Mozambique, and decided to stop at a wrecking yard for some parts I needed for my Jeep. Having salvaged them, I jumped from the hood/bonnet of a car into a rusty nail which penetrated my heel to a maximum depth. It was terribly painful and the next morning a red blood line appeared from the heel all along my leg to my groin. My mother was very concerned and advised me to see a doctor immediately. She was certain I had contacted blood poisoning. Again, I had to make a major decision, and very soon at that. To be frank, I just hated to leave my busy duties, get dressed and drive to see a doctor. So an easier decision availed itself. The healing evangelist David Nunn from America was in Johannesburg that night and I would have him pray for me. Again, I placed my faith in the promises of a living God and His servant.

God's healing power immediately went into action and when I reached Johannesburg City Hall that night the red stripe had already disappeared. I was totally healed.

Jesus said: *"When ye pray, believe that you receive it and you shall have it . . ."*

Hearing the voice of God—The big tent

In my first and young days of ministry in the missionary/evangelistic field, I desperately wanted a tent. I began to shop around, but they were all financially out of my reach. I must confess that I have never been good at fund raising nor gathering partners in my ministry. I have always felt that if God wanted partners to support me, He would send them in His own time and volition. Unfortunately this has always been a sad missing link in my life and ministry, so always without further ado, I have just gotten out and done the work with my own hands and determination. In the course of this action, I have witnessed many miracles. I have heard and acted upon God's voice many times.

I did find a tent. It was an ex-circus tent. I was told by the owner that having been through a storm, it had a few leaks but was easily reparable.

Being rolled up, I could not inspect it, so I bought it at face value. It did not have poles so I had to make my own. The price sounded reasonable, so with every penny that I could acquire, I bought it.

Upon inspection, I found the tears to be scores of feet long and was thus introduced to weeks of labor with a glove and heavy duty needle and thread. With a hacksaw, I had cut and welded all the side, middle and main poles which were twelve feet, thirty feet and forty feet, respectively. I had embarked upon a mammoth task. A circus tent, being constructed of heavy army canvas was no small business. Alone, and with my own hands, I moved the mountains of canvas and hand stitched hundreds of feet. God's grace was sufficient and I enjoyed every moment of it, anticipating the great moves of God's glory which would be revealed in it. This glory could be best described by my recent trip back to South Africa one month ago.

I had preached at a church in a town called Middleburg. Upon completion of the meeting, a man introduced himself to me and asked me if I remembered a tent campaign I conducted at a place called Vereeninging, thirty eight years ago. I assured him that I did. He remarked that in all his life of serving God, he had never been in a more anointed meeting ever. He told me that a near kin's person of his had accompanied him. She had been born with squint eyes and was instantly healed in those meetings, and that her miracle or healing remains until this day. Of course, this testimony was of great encouragement to me.

I manually worked extremely hard on that tent. I repaired the "tears." A better word would be dongas or valleys. I constructed the poles, etc., and was donated a platform which was designed to be the same as that of Oral Robert's. It was in the apartheid days, which required that the various races lived apart in their own areas and environments. This necessitated me moving the tent to all areas. I evangelized in the black areas, the then so-named colored or mixed race areas, the Indian areas and the white areas. I have always felt that the Gospel should be preached to all people of all nations and countries. Today, things have changed and it is easier to evangelize where all people can come to the tent, and not the tents go to all people. It was difficult in those days. Irrespective of my own stutter which was, thank God, undetectable when I preached, God was healing and doing great signs among the people. I advertised, "Bring the blind, the deaf, lame and dumb." In many instances, God did great signs and wonders amongst the people. Untold thousands received the baptism of the Holy Ghost, with the evidence of speaking in tongues. So many were saved and delivered.

The summer of 1971 came and went. Both Br. Reinhardt Bonnke's and my tents were moving around the country. My last crusade for the summer was being conducted at a place called Riverlea. The meetings would conclude on Sunday afternoon and the tent would be stored for the winter. There would be a great crowd in attendance and I would have all the help necessary for the dismantling and packing away of the equipment in the pantechnicon trailer. I could not understand why God told me to insure the tent a few days before the storing procedure. It definitely made more sense to me that the tent should have been insured while I was using it. I mentioned this reasonable concern to God and all He said was "Don't argue; do it!" I did not have any money to insure it, so went to the bank, took a loan and so made my way to the insurance company, and concluded the deal on the Friday.

Sunday afternoon was the final meeting and the tent was jam packed to capacity. I would make an announcement requesting volunteers to help with the dismantling, on conclusion of the meeting. It was a great disappointment to me when shortly before the meeting ended; the tent was drenched in a downpour of rain. The canvas would now have to dry before packing and storing. I would now have to come in, find labor and so pack it away for the winter. I returned home disappointed with the turn of circumstances.

At six o'clock the next morning, I received a call from the convening pastor of the crusade, Chris Vandervent, informing me that the tent had been totally destroyed in a vicious storm during the night. To the best of my knowledge, South Africa has only had two tornados, and this was one of them. The morning news and papers were full of the damages done. My tent was gone and when I arrived on the scene,

I found the canvas ripped to shreds. The 40ft steel center poles were totally severed in half, the middle poles were all bent to 180 degrees. All that remained intact were the platform, the side poles and of course the 5ft steel stakes.

The article appeared in the major newspaper, namely The Rand Daily Mail and appears here-under. I hope I learned a lesson here. Remember the king in the Bible who did not beat the arrows sufficient times on the ground and so suffered lack? If God is in your plans let's make them big! Let us listen and respond accordingly. (*2 Kings 13:15-19.*) I should have insured the tent for much more than I did but I do get a kick out of it, knowing that God pulled one on an insurance company.

An earlier experience of a very tiring trying day

I had my ex-circus tent pitched in Pretoria where we had experienced a great spiritual revival. One of the brothers approached me and offered to paint my ministries' name on the pantechnicon trailer. I gladly and appreciatively accepted his offer and left the trailer on site for several days. The crusade had come to an end and the trailer was fully packed and ready to go. The day I came to retrieve it two unpleasant surprises awaited me.

Firstly, the paint job was extremely undesirable and I could not face my name looking like some ghost train. Bless the brothers' heart for his work of love about he obviously knew nothing about sign writing, and the second surprise was that I had a flat tire so I commenced to change it. No easy task however, what with a giant pantechnicon loaded to capacity with a circus tent, poles, stakes, ropes, chairs, platform, organ, etc.

Having hydraulically jacked up the axle, removed the wheel, I was lying under the trailer, checking something when I happened to see the jack moving ever so slightly. With haste I jumped out from under the trailer—not one second too soon before it came crashing down on the ground. That day my life was literally saved by the "blink of an eye." Had I been looking elsewhere but at the jack I would surely have perished.

The day wore on and after tremendous and tedious labor, I finally had the tractor and trailer hooked and ready to go. Due to financial inadequacy I was driving an uninsured, unlicensed vehicle. I write this shamefully, but what can one do, when you've worked on a schedule advertised and by the day the tent has to be erected, God (or man) has not supplied the finances for the necessary legalities. In my mind God's work comes first—so I would get there and trust Him to see to the rest and keep me safe.

I turned onto the freeway between Pretoria and Johannesburg, and headed for home. As dusk and darkness came, I switched on the lights and to my horror found the lights to be very dim. Obviously the alternator was not charging and it would not be long before my illegal vehicle would come to a stop on the freeway. I overshot my turnoff and was now headed into the metropolitan Johannesburg. Stress, panic, and tension set in. After an attempted U-turn, over the medium, my driving wheels came off the ground and I was hanging in mid-air. By some miracle I backed up and continued, but decided to take the first exit and park on some side street for the night. That's what I did but happened to choose some *"cul de sac"*, dead end with posh houses. With no place to park, I tried to turn around. The engine stalled and failed to start. I had now jack knifed and blocked the whole road. How would the people get to work the next morning?

Now I needed to get help from somewhere and walked to a house to try and make a phone call. (How fortunate we are today to have cell phones!) I'm afraid the "good old days" were not so good! Well, when the good man of the house opened the door and I tried to speak, all I could do was stutter. The stress had taken its toll! For some unknown reason the man broke into uncontrollable fits of laughter. He could not stop! I was devastated! I walked away and cannot clearly remember how I called my ex-wife who came and picked me up and took me home, where I would try to get some rest after an arduous, awful day. Was I now experiencing the same trials as the apostle Paul as God's word said to Ananias?

"I will show him how great things he must suffer for my names' sake." (Acts 9:16)

When I returned the next morning I was appalled to see the truck and trailer surrounded by officers of the Law, who just got into their cars and left the scene. Phew! Thank you Jesus! How I ever got that "circus" mobile and back home, I cannot and do not care to remember.

1972

My call as pastor to Sabie

Shortly after, I departed for my annual hunting trip in Mozambique, after which I planned to spend an extensive time (40 days) in fasting and prayer in the African Bush. After three days, God answered my prayer and told me to end the fast. The same day after arriving home, I became deathly ill.

That night my fever reached 106 degrees. Every beat of my heart felt as if my head would explode from pain. I had been bitten by a tick and had contacted tick fever. I lost one fifth of my body weight in five days. If I did not have the in-home necessary care, and still been out in the African bush, I would surely have died. While in this delirium, I received a vision from God. I was no stranger to dreams, visions and revelations. They had become a part of my life and ministry.

In the vision, I saw the Taj Mahal in India and looking over the walls, I saw someone in a priestly like form. I called to him and asked him to show me the palace. He answered and said. "No, but I will show you something else," and took me down into a basement. Herein I saw all manner of snakes, lizards, serpents, etc., interspersed with old greasy dirty logs. I felt this place should be set on fire and commenced in the art of fire making by boring a spinning stick into the dirty, greasy log. Every time some smoke and little flame would begin, it would die again. Suddenly God spoke to me and said, "John, as the Taj Mahal is the most beautiful in India, so I send you to the most beautiful place in South Africa, but the sin is great and you will not easily get my fire to burn. But persist, and I will send a revival that place has never, and never will again, have." At that very moment, the phone rang and the district superintendent of our organization requested if I would take the vacant assembly in a little town called

Sabie. I relayed a positive answer and within a month, I found myself the pastor of this little church.

Sabie is nestled in a valley beneath majestic Mount Andersen, one of the highest points in South Africa. Surrounded by forests, waterfalls, mountains and valleys, it surely is the most beautiful area of South Africa. In the three years I was there, the church grew abundantly. We truly enjoyed great revival. While my calling has never truly been that of a pastor, I viewed my pastoring to be a training field for myself. As an evangelist and revivalist, I had to learn to affiliate myself with the very real problems which pastors and their wives and family endure.

Collision into train diverted

Whist pastoring the Sabie assembly of the Full Gospel Church of God in South Africa, I also served satellite towns such as Lydenburg, Blyderivier, Graskop, etc. In the main road of Graskop was a railroad crossing. There were no lights or boons to warn pedestrians. Usually a big sign displaying STOP, LOOK AND LISTEN was posted at railroad crossings in little country towns. I remember none of this at Graskop.

It was late, I had finished my pastoral duties and an extremely heavy mist enveloped the area. It would be a long and dangerous trip home to Sabie. I would be driving along a winding mountain road home.

Whilst driving toward the railroad crossing I noticed strange flickering lights ahead of me. Any thought of the crossing never entered my mind. I was only concerned about getting home, and as I was about to pass the lights, I was immediately confronted by sudden danger. A train was crossing the road and the moving wheels interspersed the lights of a parked car on the opposite side. Applying urgent full brake my car came to a stop a few inches from the wheels. I quickly reversed and was very thankful for the lights of the parked car at that late hour in a very remote little country town. While in Sabie, God blessed me with a pre-world War II airplane and hereunder, I recall various adventures with Fairchild:

PV ZS BAM

The aircraft belonged to a flight engineer and one of my kin members. They took much pride in it and renovated it to the state of real beauty. Once, when someone was helping me to push it, he took out his handkerchief, put it between his hand and the strut, and said, "It's a sin to put your bare hands on an aircraft like this!" I suppose one of my mistakes in life was that I never had her entered in an air show. ZS BAM would surely have taken first place.

My first drama came on a landing. I had been doing circuits and bumps with the instructor and due to some misunderstanding, he was expecting me to do the actual landing, while I, in turn, after flying just above the runway, released the controls to him. Needless to say the aircraft was landing itself while incurring severe bumps and thus doing structural damage to the landing gear. Upon discovering that no one was in charge of landing the aircraft, I felt pretty confident that I could do it on my own and prepared myself for my first landing. Unknowingly, the tail wheel cable had suffered so much damage that it was at the breaking point and already was stationed at 90 degrees opposite to in-line landing direction. Upon touchdown, the aircraft abruptly veered off at right angles to the runway. My instructor accelerated the throttle, trying to gain air speed to clear the oncoming trees. When this proved futile, he applied hard brakes, and with no steering wheel gear, we ended up in a cloud of dust, having done a few ground loops. Much to his embarrassment and my shock, we finally came to rest safely. Thanks are to God!

Shortly after this, I was destined to experience one of my most dangerous precarious trips ever. It was the day of my transfer from one assembly to another. Not only was this really my first overland flight, but it was also an international flight and the weather and terrain was of the most trying that a young, inexperienced rookie pilot could ever endure. I had to fly along a mountain side, look for a hole in low lying cloud, attempt to circle up through it, and so clear both mountain and cloud. After hindsight reflection of thought, I realized I was given stupid advice by my instructor. My airport of departure was Sabie in the Eastern Transvaal of South Africa. Sabie lies at the foot of the Drakensberg mountain chain of South Africa with an elevation of some 2000 feet. Not five miles away as the crow flies is Mount

Andersen towering more than 8000 feet. Along the sides of this berg are many towering dangerous mountain peaks. I was endeavoring to climb through low lying cloud for some seven thousand feet. I was not instrument rated, had never been in cloud before, did not know what to expect and to add severe strain and stress, I had Galilee my little girl of four years of age as an accompanying passenger. It would have been so much wiser and safer to have first flown east, away from the mountain to the low veld of less than 1000 feet and then tried to ascend. Not only would I probably have found blue skies but would most certainly have eliminated the low lying clouds and mist which gathers at the foot of the mountain.

Before continuing with my story, let me state that I later learned from discussing this subject with more experienced fliers that I had been in the fatal "spiral of death" experience. This spinning, rotating nose dive to ground Terra firma ensures that you have limited airflow over the aircraft controls. As best remembered and related with my limited knowledge, here is what happened:

After a day of tearful, nostalgic goodbyes to friends, loved ones and assembly members at the little ground strip airport, I buckled up myself and most loved little daughter and amidst many hand waves, tears and smiles, took off. I headed north along the foot of South Africa's second most high mountain peak and range. Meandering through mountain low lying mist and cloud, I searched for the promised blue hole. Off to my left and west, lay the steep sides of the berg, no more than a mile away. Having found a promise of blue skies, I commenced my upward spiral approach through cloud. I suppose I must have ascended some 1000 feet when total cloud enclosed me and I became totally enveloped and disorientated, not knowing which way is up, sideways or downward. I quickly switched my attention to my limited knowledge of instruments. I was flying V.F.R (Visual Flight Rules) and needed a constant view of ground to orientate my flight. I was now en-wrapped in total mist and cloud. My first perception was that my airspeed was well above normal level flight speed. I was therefore in a dive. I pulled back on the stick and my compass began gyrating. The aircraft was obviously not in level mode but in a banked position. The slip and slide ball was off to one side max at one time. The airspeed and compass gyrations accelerated in intensity. I did not know what to do. By pulling back on the stick, I had pulled the aircraft into a tight, downward spiral. Speed increased, compass gyrations increased. Slip and slide ball was off to one side. I was in the spiral of death with no airflow over my controls. Galilee, my little daughter and I were less than 186 seconds away from a fiery violent death crash. There was nothing I could do but only what the apostle Peter did when he began sinking in the boisterous sea. Out of my heart and mouth came a wrenching passionate call. Jesus! God help us! And let it be stated categorically, unequivocally and undoubtedly—in my severity of intense panic, God came into that aircraft, put his hands on mine and brought that aircraft under control. Only experienced fliers are capable of knowing the extremity of this miraculous saving miracle.

Consider the following: Twenty minutes after take-off and having flown many miles north, I was again seen battling in cloud above town and airport. Consider again, I finally cleared cloud at 14,000 feet, only 2000 feet lower than the maximum ceiling of my prewar World War II aircraft. Not only did it feel like hours but there is no way that I could have been enveloped in cloud for less than half an hour. When God came and took over and helped me, a great peace came into me and every instrument began functioning properly. Consider again, the higher you fly, the thinner the air, the slower your rate of ascent. By scientific facts and my own estimation of time, I do believe that I was flying blind in cloud, for anything between forty minutes and an hour. God enabled a totally novice rookie pupil pilot to become instrument rated in a few minutes, a far cry from the 186 seconds to your death when in the spiral of death. My heart goes out to many bush pilots who were not as fortunate as me. This pernicious story does not end yet for I was destined to a three prong attack finally culminating with the most hazardous and dangerous experience still ahead. Attack number two came upon breaking cloud at 14,000 feet. I was now well above Mount Andersen's 8000 plus foot peak and well above the low lying mist of relief rain packed on the seaward side of the Drakensberg, but now I found myself flying through tunnels of severe cumulus nimbus, commonly known as "Charlie Bravo" thunder clouds. To the left and right, lightning was flashing within the walls of the cloud tunnels. Thunder and turbulence was terrible. Little did I know that if I was caught in an updraft, I would finally be spewed out of this thunder/lightning cloud at 30,000 plus feet. That of course would be a total impossibility because I am given to understand that even modern passenger jets would not enter these clouds for fear of disintegration amidst the severe updrafts and downdrafts of 200 mph wind shear and rocks of speeding ice.

While flying through this tunnel, it suddenly occurred to me that I could go up no further and what would I do if the tunnel ended around the next corner. Man, it was a no-brainer to know that this aircraft has now got to reach a much lower elevation in the minutest of time. All that was needed was a joystick to be pushed forward and presto! Downward we went into rain and poor visibility. Nevertheless, good old Planet Earth's surface could be seen and so amongst rain, semi-darkness and wind, we covered some 300 miles to Naboomspruit, where we landed safely on a ground strip. That night, sitting at home with my parents and brother, experiencing the aftershock of the severest nerve shocks that any given day could bring forth in one's life, I asked to join them for a stiff brandy or whatever they were drinking. I badly needed my nerves to settle. Fortunately, or unfortunately, I do not know, but my brother declined my request, knowing the effects which hard liquor might bring on a young preacher who had no former taste of alcohol. After thanking God for the spared life of myself and daughter, and having tucked Galilee into her bed, I too, got into bed where, sweet slumber, the balm of crippled spirits would revive my body, soul and spirit to awake to another day.

Whilst I slept, I was totally unaware of a great spiritual battle ensuing in the heavens at that very moment. Satan, the prime prince of evil, calamity and death, was strategically placing his angels, demons, principalities and powers to wipe Galilee and I off the earth. Sometime that night in fretful sleep, I must have awaked and for a fleeting moment felt the panic, stress and dilemma of intense fear and helplessness that I had so recently experienced. That feeling, however, would quickly have disappeared in the face of reality that I was now laying on a bed of safe repose. Galilee, my daughter of four was also safe to face her future life. Not only was Satan moving his forces on the chessboard of our lives, but little be-known to ourselves, so too was God. A kind, loving and good God was also at work to preserve the lives of two of His choice servants. At that precise moment God was strategically placing his angels with premeditated thoughts and plans for the preservation of John and Galilee Hitchcock's' lives.

When morning came, we arose to be greeted by a beautiful sunny day. Said of old, "The woes of death have passed," however I did not know that the sword of death was nearer than ever. We departed on our first international flight from Naboomspruit South Africa to Fort Victoria, Rhodesia, where this day would make yesterday's compare to the tip of the iceberg. Satan, in hellish glee and serious mindful meditation was arranging his plan of attack. Thank God, the keeper of Israel, who neither slumbers nor sleeps states that the steps of a good man are ordered by the Lord. God always gives to us the victory in Christ Jesus.

After the normal pre-flight checks and greeting of loved ones, etc., we took off to enjoy the flight. All went well and we landed at Messina and cleared customs on the South African side. Having accomplished this, we took off, flew over the Limpopo River and landed at Beitbridge on the Rhodesian side. It was midday and what should have been about half an hour to clear customs and thereafter a two hour flight to Fort Victoria, finally culminated in a whole afternoon of ordeal.

The woes began when there was no customs officer at the little post. Office locked no phones, no transport to the little town, no aviation fuel to refill the tanks. To avoid being illegal in the country, we waited, hoping that a customs and immigration agent would come along. Hour after hour passed but no one came, and when the time was exhausted, we finally left, hoping that we could rectify the situation with the police at Fort Victoria. There was now barely enough time to reach our destination before dark. Severe weather was brooding.

During the flight, we encountered four severe thunder storms and were forced to circumvent them. The turbulence on the outer rim of the storm was so severe that I was seized with fear that a wing would break off.

Considering that the aircraft was constructed of wood and fabric and was more than forty years old, my fears were justified. At one stage, we were seized by an updraft and with full throttle in a downward dive; we were still ascending at a horrific rate. After these episodes of extreme turbulence, I never again doubted the ability of that old aircraft to perform under any condition.

At 6:00 PM we were over Lake Kyle and should have touched down at Fort Victoria within the next half hour. The only problem was that a severe storm was now directly over Fort Victoria. We would have to circumvent this one as well. It would be suicide to fly into the storm. I turned around hoping to get in the back way before dark. What I did not know was that this was no isolated storm but was the upstart of a "front," meaning the storm was now hundreds of miles in diameter. It turned out to be the worst storm Rhodesia had experienced since 1907.

As far north as Salisbury, the whole country was now under an electric blackout. The whole country's power was knocked out. Night was soon to be upon us and the severe storm added to the blackness. Keep in mind, this is Africa. This is bush country! No settlement for hundreds of miles. No beacons, no lights, no fuel, no radio, no nothing, but primitive bush and mountains. The rain and mist was now pressing us down into the valleys. Lightning was striking constantly. Thunder claps were deafening. Fuel was a critical factor. The gauge was on empty and there was no way into town which would never be seen anyway, due to the power failure. The inverted Ranger engine with the oil pan on top was beginning to make strange noises most probably due to lack of oil. I was now in survival mode, trying to clear every little hill. It was now almost totally dark. Visibility was quickly failing.

I have always been well geographically and directionally minded and this definitely played its part in saving my life on that fitful day. On my former safaris into Mozambique, I knew that the main road from Fort Victoria traveled directly east to Umtali. I was east of Fort Victoria trying to head north and had to fly over this road. This now became our only hope and Galilee and I began intense prayer to just reach this road. When we finally did, it was of little consolation. It was too narrow. Trees on either side actually met in the middle of the road. Heading west toward Fort Victoria I finally found a construction area where a bridge was being built. Although the distance was very short, I might just be able to bring the aircraft down here. I made immediate plans to land. The old aircraft was not equipped with landing lights and visibility was now an extreme factor. On final approach and full flap flying just more than stalling speed, I clearly heard the voice of God speaking to me. He said: "John, trust me and fly into that storm." So I did, and guided myself as best I could by flying over the road, being guided by the random lights of cars. God was faithful to his command and I experienced minimal rain on the windshield. It was as if He created a rainless tunnel for me in the middle of that rainstorm. Even the turbulence ceased.

My greatest consolation throughout this horrific experience was the knowledge that my new assembly members would be gathered in intense prayer for me. Apart from the fear of danger, death and destruction, a father's heart was for the life of his child. Galilee's safety was of major importance to me. As I flew down the windless, rainless tunnel with extreme critical shortage of fuel and oil, a great peace came over me and I knew we would make it for the reception and arrive safe. In later weeks, I was shocked to see a high antenna right next to the road. Again, God's safekeeping insured that we did not strike it. God is so good. Life could have ended for us those 34 years ago. God obviously had need for us and those 34 years were filled with labor for Him. Galilee is now married to Gary Guess and together they labor for God and she has become an evangelist of most notable significance.

We were now flying in total darkness and ahead of us was a greater conglomeration of car lights. We were definitely approaching Fort Victoria. I had no clue where the airport was situated. I had hoped to find it in daylight with radio support. We now had none of that. Earlier a Vickers Viscount passenger airline had seen us battling through the valleys and mist and had informed Salisbury air traffic control of our predicament. In those days it was not compulsory to file a flight plan, so I did not avail myself of this benefit, thinking that it would just add further stress to our flight. Had I done it, we might have been benefited with a customs agent, and thereby landed well ahead of nightfall.

Still several miles ahead of Fort Victoria by God's providence, I looked down and happened to see the passing white lines of the runway. God had led us directly over the airport, which was in total blackout. As best I could, I found the end of the runway, circled back, disciplined myself to be exceedingly careful, telling myself a hasty landing could be fatal at the very end of a severe testing. Consider my predicament, a young novice pilot, on his first overland flight. No radio and due to my stutter, a terrible fear to even talk over it. No landing lights, no lit airstrip, no knowledge of the runway or wind direction. Nor air traffic control. The severest weather since 1907 resulted in a countrywide electrical blackout. No airport to deviate to and 250 miles any way of nothing but bush. This was 1973 and Africa at its worst on a bush pilot. This was Satan's game plan at its best. However, like Peter of old, my church was at the airport gathered in constant prayer for us. God gives to us the victory every time. Hallelujah!

To make matters worse, the aircraft was a "tail dragger," meaning the steering wheel is situated at the rear of the aircraft. On a scale of one to ten, the difficulty in landing a tail dragger compared to a nose wheel is ten to one. Now the final test was upon me and with God's help, I landed that aircraft without runway or landing lights in the blackest night and came to a perfect stop. One of the most difficult of times to keep my composure was when I stopped and exited the airplane. My whole being wanted to fall on the ground, kiss it and weep from the depths of my heart, but could not because there were many of my new assembly members and I had to keep my composure. The final proof of God's miraculous safekeeping providence came the next morning. I was called by air traffic control to collect my aircraft, where the wind had blown it down the length of the entire runway to the farthest fence. On taxing back down the runway, the aircraft ran out of fuel, and no oil showed on the dipstick.

The only sour note to this whole episode came when I was interviewed by the local newspaper. The article made front page headlines and though I gave God all the glory, the title read: "Pilot Saved by Providence. The article appears hereunder.

Closing note: Rhodesia is now called Zimbabwe. Fort Victoria is now Masvingo and Salisbury, Harare.

ZS-BAM—another adventure—faith or fate?

Months later, we returned to visit my parents at Naboomspruit. This time we had no problems with weather or customs, but a problem did arise shortly before landing. Smoke began entering the cockpit. We landed safely and upon investigation, I found that the number one cylinder had cracked to reveal a 1/8" crack which circulated halfway around the cylinder pot. These pots are not encased in a block like a car. They are air cooled and therefore each one of the six cylinders is exterior and independent. Spares for this pre-world War II aircraft were exceedingly scarce or worse, still, literally unobtainable. I needed a cylinder pot. And having one at home I decided to fly by faith back to Fort Victoria for repairs.

In hindsight, I view my faith move as most optimistic and bordering on stupidity. When the propeller was turned, the piston could be seen moving through the crack of the cylinder. How could one risk your life in attempting many hours of flight under these conditions? My faith said it could be done but it did not quite work out as I anticipated. Not long after takeoff, the aircraft went into a violent shudder and oil covered the windshield. Fortunately the engine still functioned and I was able to turn around and make a safe landing. As a note of humor, I remember remarking to God, "Where do we land God?" Well, He sure did ensure that airport was not too far away.

Damages now proved to be much worse. The whole cylinder pot had disintegrated, causing total loss of cylinder, piston, rings and con-rod. Except for the rings I did have everything at home, so my father drove me there to collect them. This aircraft was classified under certain conditions where it could be worked on privately so I was within legal conditions to do my own repairs. As it happened, I met a former girlfriend of mine and her husband, and he being a technician, offered to help me do the repairs. The rings were unobtainable but he said that they looked exactly like a Fordson Tractor and explained to me where I could obtain these in neighboring Pietersburg, now called Polokwane. I got lost and landed up at a wrecking yard and promptly gave the attendant the old piston and requested him to try and find me some rings which would fit the piston.

After all avenues failed to supply the necessary rings, I despondently headed home. Being well out of town, I remembered the old piston and really wanted to keep it as a trophy of my faith, I turned around and headed for the wrecking yard and arriving there just before closing, I was greeted by a jubilant attendant stating that he had found "just the thing." They came from an old Packard which had been parked in the yard for a long time.

Upon delivering them to my technician friend, he too assured me that they were "just the thing." A few hours later, we were flying again and as long as I had the airplane, cylinder #1 had a better compression and burned whiter and cleaner that any of the other five.

God had again come through in his own wonderful way to reward my faith, of fate? Ironically, I had never met my technician friend before and never saw him again. God supplied him just at the right time! I know this is not coincidence but certainly assures me that "they who are led by the Spirit are the sons of God."

ZS BAM Fairchild Ranger

1973 TO 1975

Another close call with ZS BAM

During the years that I pastored in Fort Victoria, Rhodesia, I had to speak at a conference in a distant town called Gwelo. It was a weekend meeting. After all these years, I still remember the title "Break up your fallow ground." It was an outstanding meeting, ending with many souls consecrating and rededicating their hearts and lives to Jesus. This was on Saturday night.

After ministering the Sunday night in Gwelo I was scheduled to speak at the High School opening assembly at Fort Victoria. Some 600 children would attend, while the principle and staff would assemble on the platform behind me. It was an important meeting.

Due to the distance and time element we had chosen to fly rather than drive and so very early on Monday morning we were committed to the airport which consisted of a grassy, ground strip. Our party consisted of my youth leader Yan Venter, I, our wives and our children CJ (Jaco,) Reynette and Galilee. It had been a very rainy weekend resulting in a drenched airstrip housing many puddles of water. The sky was thick with low cloud. It was about 6:00am with the sun not yet up and our flight would be about an hours' duration. My next very important assignment would be shortly after 8:00am. Driving was not an alternative. We had to fly. So after the pre-flight checks we lined up for take-off. The Fairchild ZS BAM was a tail dragger, meaning that as the aircraft gains speed the tail is first lifted from the ground and then as speed is increased, take-off is initiated. Being familiar with the aircraft's acceleration I became instantly nervous. The wheels were bogging down in the mud hindering take-off speed and the tail could just not be elevated. I called for everybody to lean forward as far as possible. With every take-off there is a PNR (point of no return.) Having passed this point we were now committed. We were quickly reaching the end of the runway, terminating with a fence, beyond which a high line of electric pylons crossed our path in a semi-circle around the airfield. I now realized that clearing the fence would be an obstacle in itself but clearing the pylons would be impossibility.

Having now reached the end of the runway the "acid test" was inevitable. I knew we had not reached take-off speed, but with God's help we would make it. Man I can see in my spirit's eye, God bellowing a command to his angels—Go and help my saints! (Hebrews 1:13, 14) and I can see "angels wings" coming under ours for lift-off. We "groaned" over the fence and now approached the pylons. Clearing them was impossible so I had to do a 45-60 degree turn within them. This turn would result in a slip and slide condition with gravity having the upper hand. A very tight turn towards port now required me to keep one eye on the edge of the wing and the other on the pylons. We were now turning within the semi-circle. The wing could not be lifted more than one yard (meter) off the ground and we had to complete a 180 degree turn. During the course of this turn I doubt if we rose more than an inch. Upon leveling out we were able to gain speed and so gain height. "Wow," but we had not reached our destination yet! We had to weave through low laying cloud upon descent but God was with us. I made the meeting and uncompromisingly I made an alter call with some 75 children and four teachers rising from their seats to receive Jesus as their savior.

I reckon this altar call challenge resulted in some serious embarrassment amongst the staff because prior to my next turn at conducting service at assembly the principal called me in and very diplomatically said: "Pastor Hitchcock, when the Catholic priest holds his meeting, he kindly leaves his robes at home—would you please be so kind as not to conduct an altar call." Of course I adhered to his wishes knowing there is a time to sow and a time to reap. I would sow and the Holy Spirit would reap in His own good time. Recently Yan visited with us on the boat and mentioned a further fact that I had forgotten. Upon leaving Gwelo, I found that only one wheels' brake was functioning. This caused a very severe problem on both take-off and landing because applying brake would cause a ground-loop. Again—on takeoff we were committed and on landing "hope for the best . . ." Yan said I told him of this dilemma only after landing.

I later used the above mentioned incident many times as an illustration in my preaching. Indeed I even preached an entire message on it. Consider a 5 point outline:

Title—Committed
Introduction—No cancellation of our assigned duty.
Body: 1. Trust in God
           2. Point your nose into the wind
           3. Commit yourself and cross the point of no return
           4. Know that God will do His part
           5. Complete your mission
(Psalm 34: 4, 6, 7, 9, 10, 15, 17-19)

You preachers can figure out the other details. End with some verses like—young lions chapter, trust in the Lord, do exploits.

I now know why so many singing artists and others have been killed in light aircraft crashes—when duty calls and arrangements having been made—one is committed. Satan being the prince of the power of the air is able to use the weather as his tool. Thank God however for His protection over his saints for Hebrews 1:13, 14 say that God disposes of angels to minister to them who are heirs of salvation.

"There shall no evil befall thee for he shall give his angels charge over thee to keep thee in all thy ways. They shall bear thee up in their hands, less thou dash thy foot against a stone." (Psalms 91:10-12)

At the time of this writing my good friend and colleague Rev. Yan Venter is shopping for an airplane after having totaled his former one in a crash with "good old Mother Earth."

I recall a very vivid story I once heard. It goes something like this:

A ship was en route along the Canadian shore when a voice beamed on the radio advising a turn to starboard followed by a reply.

No—you turn to starboard.
No—you turn.
You don't understand this is the Battleship HMS—whatever
No—you don't understand—This is a lighthouse
No further arguments—dispute settled—case closed.

I win the rodeo championships

Up to the year 1973 and my 33 years of age I cannot recollect that I had ever heard or known of a rodeo. I do not think there was ever such an event in South Africa or Rhodesia.

I was pastoring in Fort Victoria, Rhodesia, Yan was my youth leader and we were busy at the local fair. The youth department of our church was running a booth, giving out Bibles, tracts, etc. It was a big event and many people attended. As I was meandering through the crowds I saw the most unbelievable sight. In mid-air a man was being propelled 15 feet through the air. Man this was my scene!

Upon arrival at the scene my eyes were introduced to the arena of erected poles, big Rhodesian bulls and would be riders for the grand prize of 300 Rhodesian dollars. Don't laugh too loud because the Rhodesian dollar was equal to approximately three American dollars and that was the year 1973. It was quite a desired prize. What a tragedy and disgrace to the current Zimbabwe (changed name of Rhodesia) government. With the whole world boycotting Ian Smith's government, the Rhodesian dollar was one of the most powerful in the world. Since Mugabe's take-over the country slid down a toboggan slide to poverty. Probability of the highest inflation rate in history has caused them to cut off the last three zero's a number of times so that today a million dollars could not buy a loaf of bread. Shelves of stores are empty, people are hungry and poor and Mugabe lives in a home that would turn any Arabian Sheik or even King Solomon to envy.

Nevertheless in those days Rhodesia was a jewel of the British Empire. Cities were modern, safe and clean. Rhodesia was a first world country within a third world continent.

It being cattle country, be sure that the biggest prize bulls were at that fair. I stood in awe watching the riders mount those enormous animals and as the gate opened no one remained on longer than a second or two. Soon no more hopeful prize winners were willing to mount the steers, and the host began pleading saying "come on guys—we did all this erection work, got the bulls here and we need some volunteers." I cried out "Hold up guys, I've got just the right guy who will win the prize, I'll go get him, when he comes give him a big applause. His name is Yan Venter!"

John Hitchcock

I ran back to our booth and said "Yan come here, I've got just the right thing for you to raise money for the youth project." Yan later told me he eyed me with suspicion. Something was wrong here. Upon arrival everybody cheered Yan. He was told to mount the steer and win the prize.

Well Yan was game; he mounted, gripped that body rope with both hands and said "I am ready." I was watching his knee which was caught behind the post—(shame on me that I didn't warn him) so when the gate opened and that bull came out with vengeance, Yan was scooped off even before he was out of the gate. My voice boomed—Not fair, not fair, give him another chance, his knee was behind the post! Yan gallantly mounted his second bull with deliberation; made sure he was clear and said "open that gate." I held my breath and saw Yan was doing better than any previous competitor. I counted a full 5 seconds when Yan was bucked into the air and hit the ground with vehemence. Everybody cheered and I was laughing profusely. It was then that the crowd turned on me saying, "OK big mouth, your turn next."

"No said I, I've just come off the pulpit and still have my preaching suit on." Upon their urging I soon found myself, best preaching suit and all striding that bull. Having seen those rides I knew what to expect. This bull is going to turn into a bullet exiting a muzzle when this gate opens, I thought.

Nobody knew anything about one hand riding as I have subsequently seen here in America, so I got hold of that rope with vengeance, tried to hook my toes under his belly but was quickly aware that his girth was too broad, nevertheless I tried. All I knew, bring hell or high water, I am sitting this bull until I get off by myself. The gate opened and I was subjected to the roughest adrenalin ride of my life. It felt like minutes and probably was.

After a while the bull came to a standstill and honored my victory with a loud—boohoo! I jumped off and walked off with $300 to add to the youth's financial drive.

Myself with long term friend Yan Venter

Bilharzia, the feared African disease

When I began hunting crocodiles, I was very aware of the threat of contacting bilharzia. This parasite, when one enters low veld and tropical rivers of Africa, enters the blood stream under the toe, fingernails and skin. It then lays its eggs and so the disease spreads worms of one centimeter long, derived from snails, infests the body. It is a slow march to death. In later years, one begins passing blood and then the disease has passed to an advanced stage.

During the process one becomes constantly tired and lethargic. During those years (1966) there was no remedy of healing. I was told that only if one contacts malaria, you may experience healing due to the high fever killing the bilharzia germs. So what was I to do? Wear gum boots and water resistant clothing? No sir—too much hassle! Again, my faith in an all-powerful God who keeps His word and promises kicked into gear. "God said it; I believe it and that settles it." The Bible states:

"Greater is He that is in you than he that is in the world . . . and If the same spirit which rose Christ from the dead dwell in you, He shall quicken (make alive) your mortal body . . ."

So I told God that without any worry, I would be entering those rivers, lakes and dams and that I believe no harm would come to me. So without any further thought on the matter, that is exactly what I did.

Some six years later however, whilst I was pastoring the church in Fort Victoria, Rhodesia, I seemed to be constantly tired. I was advised that I possibly had contacted bilharzia and should have tests done. Having complied, I visited the doctor for the results, and will never forget his words: "Pastor Hitchcock, what cure did you have?" "I've had none." I responded. "Well said he, this is an amazing phenomena, because you certainly did have bilharzia but by some mystifying cure, the tests reveal that only dead bilharzia eggs lie dormant in your blood stream." Again, "They that place their trust in the Lord shall not be ashamed . . ."

As I write this, I am reminded of another similar experience.

Bossie

Bossie was a mongoose that was caught while I and a deacon named Charles Devine was out hunting. Charles later became a pastor. Being well over six feet tall, every part of his well-built, enormous frame was all muscle. Being very athletic he was able to catch a young mongoose before I did. The mongoose was a "young adult" and therefore never became completely tame. He could never be handled. Nevertheless, he settled on the parsonage property which was shared with the church. He became king of his domain. I once watched him rip the nose of a German shepherd apart as the dog tried to get hold of him once through the fence and another time under my car. The rest of the one acre property was not fenced but Bossie knew the boundaries. Bossie nightly made his bed behind the fridge when he was done patrolling his domain during the day.

We had a wonderful child of God helper by the name of Laetitia. This black lady was such a great asset. One night while I was asleep, I was awakened by Laetitia calling and knocking at the window. I was informed that Bossie had gotten into her bed and would not allow her to get into it. It took gloved hands and a thick towel to escort him to the fridge!

One Saturday, the town had a rat-race festival—whatever that meant. I was leaving for the bank and happened to see Bossie at the front wheel of my car before I left. Upon arrival at the bank I saw him running on the side walk. He had obviously climbed into the suspension system somewhere and "stowed" himself there. The rat-race festival turned into a real event as the pastor was chicken chasing his beloved pet through street and sidewalk. It was quite an event. I wonder why I didn't inform the local newspaper. They would have liked the story and thereby our church would have received free advertising.

Laetitia was a wonderful woman of prayer and during my ex-wife and my frequent "disagreements," Laetitia would be offset into a tantrum of verbal weeping and fervent prayer resulting in a sudden dispersal of the "disagreement." What did it all help—we still ended up in divorce?

One day, upon arriving home I found Laetitia in one of these "modes" and upon asking what the problem was I was informed that Bossie's hind leg had been bitten and broken off by a bull terrier. What apparently happened was that a lady was walking her dog on the side walk past our house and Bossie felt that his domain was being invaded and so attacked the dog—and of all things the dog being a BULL TERRIER! The lady had managed to get the dog off Bossie. I checked the mongoose and found the hind leg bone totally severed above the knee. Bossie was crying and in much pain. Laetitia and I got into immediate prayer and instantly Bossie quit crying although he walked favoring the leg. Three days later he was again his old self. The Bible says *"Believe on the Lord Jesus Christ, and thou shalt be saved, and thy house."* (*Acts 16:31*) The full meaning of the little word "saved" means saved and healed—spirit, soul and body! That evening the lady came to tell us that her dog, the bull terrier, was "spending the night" at the vet and I would have to foot the bill. Sure I did.

Bossie the courageous and audacious mongoose

Was he an angel?

When I pastored at Sabie, I purchased two lots at Morlothi Park being a private game reserve on the border of the Kruger National Park. The two parks were separated by the Crocodile River and a fence. In this park, I would build a home for myself.

As mentioned elsewhere God changed my plans in one night by speaking to me by the anointing. I was in the midst of big plans and endeavors whilst pastoring the Sabie assembly. I had been given a beautiful lot by my good friends Daantjie and Tinkie Kilian. I had the plans drawn and completed to build a double story thatch roof home. I was ready to embark upon the project.

I had already completed half of the building of a hanger for my airplane, and plans were underway for a new church. By morning these plans were old and obsolete. God told me to go and pastor the vacant church in Fort Victoria, (Rhodesia) now Zimbabwe. I was one of seven pastors who applied for the position, but as God had directed, I was elected so together with my family and Yan Venter and his family we very soon found ourselves in another country.

I was at this assembly some two years when an evangelist came to conduct some meetings and God told me to donate the two stands to him. Having done so, God had a return blessing for me.

About this time Yan, who was Youth leader, director and singer in our band, and I were praying together. I believe it was during November of 1973 when God told me to tell Yan that he would be in full time ministry come December 1ˢᵗ, 1973. This seemed strange as Yan had not yet completed his theological studies, neither appeared before the necessary boards of the "powers that be."

Shortly after, I was enjoying a siesta on the couch, and my ex-wife was doing the same in the bedroom. Again, God came and talked to me saying: *"Leave for America and take your wife and child with you,"* so under much excitement I woke her and said: *"Do you know where were going?"* *"To America,"* she said. I was amazed.

True to my old self of hasty excitement and "leaping before I look," I purposed to leave within two weeks and began inquiring about the cost of airfares. I had no ready cash money so I purposed to begin by selling my car. A mistake! God had His own plans and talked to a lady unknown to me who owned a cattle ranch some 180 kilometers south of Fort Victoria.

God told Anne Hodges to attend the Full Gospel Church of God in Fort Victoria that coming Sunday. When she arrived she asked God to show her why he had sent her and when I announced to the extremely surprised assembly that we would be leaving for America the following Sunday and Yan Venter would be their new pastor in the interim, God talked to Anne to pay our air-tickets.

After service this gracious lady cornered me under a tree with her check book in hand asking me how much I needed for the airfares. Stupidly, due to I suppose financial embarrassment and to ease the burden of her purse, I said, *"Well I will be selling my car for which I expect X-money and so for the tickets I will still need X amount."* Without further ado she wrote the check much to my gratitude and ease of stress.

The selling of my car resulted in arriving near an hour late for my flight which was waiting just for my family. Whilst checking in and being in a flabbergast of haste and nervousness, the agent said "Relax Rev Hitchcock. The aircraft is waiting just for you and will not leave till you're all aboard. Those must have been the "GOOD OLD TIMES" or what? Needless to say I could detect the agitation in every passenger's eye as I walked down the aisle.

Another detrimental effect of my faithless, stupid, hasty remark to Anne was that on my return after nine months to America, God led us to immediately leave for Gordons Bay in the Cape, and I had no car. Once at the Cape I could only acquire a used Volkswagen with which I had to make do for a number of years. I could still have enjoyed my nice Ford Capri Coupe.

So en route to America, having left Salisbury (Harare) International Airport we landed in Johannesburg to spend some days with our families before departure.

It was a big day when we left for the airport to commence our flight to America with a stopover in Rio De Janeiro, Brazil, where we would spend some days enjoying a vacation. All our family members came to see us off and to say the least we felt proud and honored. Here, a South African Evangelist leaving for the big land of America! Everybody wished us success.

A severe embarrassing problem surfaced when I tried to check in. The aircraft was full and there was no place for us due to the fact that our reservations had lapsed. I showed the agent the tickets, pointed to the OK and advised him that there was some error. He asked me if I confirmed my flight at least two days prior to departure. I said, "No, I did not know I had to. My booking agent did not inform me about this procedure." "That's your problem," he said. Your seats have been forfeited. I said, "Well can you put us on standby?" He pointed to a bunch of people and said: "They're all waiting on standby, nineteen of them."

So now every demon from hell began screaming in my mind. "What a fool you've been made of! You will return home with your family! Idiots—where will you get money for new tickets?" Etc. I called my brother Tony aside who was employed as a security officer of sorts at the airport and shared my embarrassment with him in privacy. He wandered off and came back sometime later saying there is nothing he can do.

All this time, I was doing spiritual warfare in my mind, rebuking the devil, speaking to this mountain of impossibility to be lifted and cast into the ocean of oblivion. In my mind I was speaking in tongues, giving the Holy Spirit opportunity to pray for me and come to my aid.

"For he that speaketh in an unknown tongue speaketh not unto men, but unto God: for no man understandeth him: howbeit in the Spirit he speaketh mysteries." (1 Corinthians 14:2)

I walked back to the agent and again inquired about the possibility of boarding that aircraft. He said, "No, sorry."

At that very moment a tall man in a brown suit walked up behind the counter and said to the agent in no uncertain terms *"IF HITCHCOCK, WIFE AND CHILD IS NOT ON THAT AEROPLANE, IT'S NOT LEAVING,"* and briskly walked away. The agent called him back to complain but with a wave of his hand and arm, finalized his decision. The agent promptly issued the tickets and gave them to me. I walked back to the family as if nothing had ever happened and all was according to plan. I called Tony aside and asked him how he achieved that, but he assured me he had achieved nothing.

Was he an angel?

On leaving, my dad who was employed at South African Airways gave me the name of a friend and associate who was the South African Airways manager in Rio de Janeiro. At arrival in Rio we boarded the first taxi and said "Hotel."

He seemed to be riding around in circles with us so the first hotel I saw, I asked him to drop us off. It was night and the next morning I called my Dad's associate who inquired where we were staying. I mentioned the hotel and he said "Oh that's the hotel where all the South African Airway's crew stays. I will arrange for you free of charge." My, isn't God good and great? ALLAH AKBAR!

Not having any committed itinerary we were privileged to spend a glorious December in sunny Rio de Janeiro. It was wonderful. Rio is sure a Portuguese jewel and best of all, The Christ statue of Corcovado, tops it all!

On leaving sunny Rio, we boarded the plane for the cold Northern Hemisphere. Our trip ended in New York with a stopover in Miami. I did not know whether to disembark in Miami or New York. (Note: at the time of writing we now live aboard our boat on the Florida Keys near Miami. If I knew what I know now, my choice would have been easy and definite.

We would have chosen to disembark in Miami, without even praying. However, during flight I went to the bathroom and asked God what we should do. He clearly directed me to New York and said: I would meet a construction engineer and he would set us off in opening doors to minister.

So said and done, we landed in an icy cold New York and met the President of the Full Gospel Business Men's Fellowship who invited me to speak at the meeting scheduled the weekend. It was a powerful service and he began contacting pastors and so our nine month itinerary began which took us throughout the Eastern States of the United States as far south as Georgia. I have forgotten his name, but ironically, it was many years later whilst back in South Africa that I read his testimony in a "Voice" magazine and lo and behold—He was a construction engineer. I had never asked him about his profession and totally forgot about it.

Peril at a frozen river

What does an African know about snow and ice! Obviously nothing! It was during my first ministerial visit to Toronto, Canada, that I was visiting with a great man of God, who would later become a very close friend, his name—Ray Stevens, a fireman.

It was December, beginning of winter, and snowed up everywhere. His house, which bordered a large section of woods, was becoming too claustrophobic for me and I decided to stroll into the forest. So the dog and I decided to go for a walk.

Coming to a frozen creek of about 25' width I decided to cross it. Fortunately the dog began running on the ice and it seemed to be cracking a little and I did not feel like getting my feet wet so I found a log threw it on the ice and dispersed my weight by crawling over it.

Later, arriving back at Ray's house, I told him about it. "How could I have been so stupid, not to have told you." Ray blurted with emphasis: "The river is not solidly frozen yet, you would have fallen through, and that is not a creek it's a roaring river—you would have flowed under the ice and ended in a lake three miles away—there to be eaten by crabs!"

At another occasion on a trip with Cornelia during the summer we visited Ray again and went to look at the creek. It surely was a deep, fast flowing river having eroded the opposite bank by many, many feet during the years. It was during this trip that Ray took us to his mountain/lake home—called "the Shack," and again I decided to go for a stroll. I got to about 200 yards from the house and was attacked by a hoard of mosquitoes, the likes of which I have never experienced! I had to run back as fast as I could, swatting mosquitoes all the way. I would have been relieved of all my blood out there. Ironically, Ray was the only one who ever told me that he would never visit Africa, because of all the insects! Fortunately South Africa is a lot different to the rest of Africa.

In the neighboring country of Mozambique, Tinus and I was once returning from a hunting trip up North, when we arrived late at night in a little town called Jao Bella. For safety sake we decided to scale the wall of a wrecking yard and sleep in it. It was a terrible hot and humid night. I spent the whole night trying to avoid mosquitoes, but Tinus as usual fell asleep immediately and slept till morning. His comfortable night however added to his detriment, because a few weeks later he landed up in hospital with an extreme dose of malaria.

Shamefully, I have to admit that when I saw him lying in some sort of a MRI tunnel contraption I could not stop laughing hilariously. I suppose it was some way of feeling comfort for all the nights his snoring kept me awake!

An unforgettable visit to Calvary and empty tomb

On my first visit to the empty tomb, as I was passing thru the entrance gate, my eyes rested on the brink of a hill, slightly to my left. An incredible anointing and the presence of God came mightily upon me. I just knew it would be Calvary's Hill, and I began weeping ecstatically. Later, after reaching composure of my emotions, I asked somebody if that would be Calvary's Hill and was told that yes, it was the backside of the hill. After visiting the tomb I walked around to the front and yes, there it was—The face of a skull.

At road level there was a bus terminal and on the brink of the hill was an Arab cemetery. God had kept Calvary, where the greatest battle in world history was fought, intact—and that with an Arab cemetery. I now felt the stirrings to spend an unforgettable night with God. I would spend the night in prayer atop Calvary and in the empty tomb. I tried to gain permission from local Arabs, but my queries gained no success, so I decided to just go ahead and do it. At around midnight I walked to the backside of the hill, near the entrance gate to the tomb, but found the entrances locked. The only way of entrance would be by climbing over the wall. This would be no easy task as the wall was high so after half an hour's inspection of the wall, I decided on a likely place where I could scale the wall. I now donned a white pair of pajamas over my clothes and began the arduous task of getting over. Once on top, I now had to reach the bottom so by hanging at arm's length from the top I jumped and landed right in the middle of a thorn bush, suffering severe skin penetration and irritation. This was the beginning of a terrifying unpleasant night on Calvary's Hill. I believe God was planning to let me experience a small part of the sufferings of Jesus. I was now not only illegally in Arab dominated property but was also invading their holy sepulchers, in the middle of the night. If detected, I was sure, I would not see the morning light. I had seen what an Arab could do with a knife from under his gown, when our bus had struck a goat. The goats' throat was slit in less than a second. A fear of death dominated me. I tried to be as quiet as possible and as I walked softly through the graves, I came upon a corrugated iron shack where I concluded they stowed the grave tools, and coming around the corner I nearly fell over an unexpected dog. The dog began barking ferociously and trying to get away would pull its chain over and over again on a sheet of corrugated iron. The silence was impregnated by calamity and noise. I was convinced that should there be any cemetery security keeper nearby he would be totally aroused by now. I decided to kneel beside the graves and portray myself as in prayer. Should I be found in this position it would at least portray a spirit of respect for their dead. Whilst I was in this attitude of watching and praying another barrage of noise filled the night. This time by geese and knowing that geese were used as watchdogs in South Africa, I realized, these Arabs were very serious in maintaining safety and security in their cemetery. By this time I was in total fear and crouching low on the ground (in white pajamas mind you) I saw legs walking between the graves. I now feared the worst. Suddenly the call of a donkey sounded the night and the legs I had seen belonged to none other than the donkey. When all settled I again began prayerfully walking amongst the graves. I now asked God that by the anointing "which is truth and no lie," He would show me exactly where the cross was planted. And so as I prayerfully, zigzagerdly meandered across the hill suddenly the anointing came over me mightily. Right here, under my feet would be where the cross was planted and my Lord had suffered for me! You dear reader might not believe in this anointing stuff, but please be reminded that apart from this anointing moving me, to say unbelievable things by way of the Word of knowledge and prophecy this same anointing would move me to make world-wide trips with no means or money. This same anointing has been the powerful tool that God has used to motivate me to serious moves. Times have been that I would go to sleep at night only to be awakened by the anointing and given directive to move to a new assembly as pastor. The Bible says *"But the anointing which ye have received of him abideth in you, and ye need not that any man teach you: but as the same anointing teacheth you of all things, and is truth, and is no lie, and even as it hath taught you, ye shall abide in him."* (1 John 2:27) Today, after more than thirty years, I know, that I know, that I know that I stood on the very one square foot of planet earth where the cross was planted!

As it happened, I was now directly under a Mulberry Tree and so I decided to climb into the tree and look at the lights of Jerusalem. Once perched on the branch I began singing the song.

I've been to Calvary

"I've never travelled far around the world, I've never seen the many thrills and sights unfurled . . . but I have taken a journey of journeys . . . up Calvary's mountain there my savior to see."

However, every time I began to sing, the dog would commence his barking, fueling a renewal to my fears. I now decided I had had enough of Calvary. No wonder Jesus sweated blood and most seriously invoked God that the cup of Calvary's woe would pass from Him. This place had now become a source of dread to me and I decided to leave it as it is. The place of the battlefield of the Gods, where Jesus was the victor and Satan the defeated foe! The only problem was that I was now in the heat of this battle. It felt as if every devil in hell had now conglomerated on that hill to enforce their vengeance on me. It felt as if I had now become their target of hateful anger and revenge. It's bad enough to be in a graveyard at night, but now there was like the pangs of death within my breast. I decided to leave hastily and scale the wall into the Christian quarter of the garden tomb.

The Bible says *"Now there was a garden in the place where he was crucified and in the garden a new tomb." (John 19:41 NRSV)* The distance of a stone's throw away from the top of the fearful hill of Calvary I now with ease scaled the wall between the Arab cemetery and the Christians' most blessed place—The garden tomb where Jesus—"The first fruits from the dead arose triumphantly!"

It was now a bright night! A full, full moon shone on the white stone of the garden tomb. A worshiper in white pajamas walked awestruck to the open gate and reverently and slowly entered. The fear and danger on Calvary had now given way to total peace and safety. I was now on Christian soil and feared no danger.

I next did something that I believe extremely few people, if any had ever done. I scaled the bars which divided the actual lying down place where the Lord lay from the other half and with great humility and respect I lay down on the very place where Jesus lay, dead and buried! I cannot explain to you how my eyes became a fountain of tears and what joyous praise was uttered from my lips. After a long time of tremendous bliss whilst soaking in the presence of Jesus, I again scaled the bars and exited the tomb. On the door the words were written.

"He is not here for He is risen." (Matt 28:6)

For what it's worth let me state. It is written in the books of the Apocrypha in the book of "Esdras" of the Catholic Bible, that Jesus was head and shoulders taller than others. In the place where the Lord lay there was an additional space of at least one foot which was chopped out of the rock where the head of the deceased would lie so if it was done for Jesus, his height must have been in approximately 6'6". Note: The above experience happened at Gordons Calvary—not the fake Catholic site of the sepulcher.

Note: I cannot recollect and remember very well on what night Galilee accompanied me on this exact same experience. We again scaled the wall into the Arab graveyard and later ended it in the

Garden tomb. She was only five years of age and had accepted the Lord as her Savior some months earlier at a little church called Farmers Mill Mission in the little town of Farmers Mills in upper New York State. In her memory she remembers everything of what I have mentioned above. It may be that she was with me on this trip.

Myself at the most sacred place on earth where our Lord Jesus Christ conquered sin, the grave, hell and satan, when He arose out of that cave.

God reveals His love and appreciation to me

For many years it has always been customary for me to rise at around 4.00am and spend time with God. During these times I have always felt the presence of God descend upon me in a quick and powerful way. One night during sleep in Gordons Bay, I dreamed I had a young pet dolphin that I regularly met down at the beach, where we spent time swimming and communicating together.

During this dream I awoke and lay listening to the roar of wind outside. Only those who live in the South West Cape of South Africa can fully know the power of the "Southeaster." During the comfort of my room and bed on such a dark, stormy, windy night, God suddenly confronted me with a question. *"John, if you did have such a young dolphin pet, would you arise now, walks to the beach, and enter the cold sea to communicate with it?"* I seriously considered the question and decided that it was hardly likely to happen. God answered. *"Do you realize John, that I leave the ivory palaces of heaven every night to love and communicate with you!"* The impact hit home.

Psalms 139:7-12

"Whither shall I go from thy Spirit? Or whither
shall I flee from thy presence?
If I ascend up into heaven, thou art there: if I make
my bed in hell, behold, thou art there.
If I take the wings of the morning, and dwell
in the uttermost parts of the sea;
Even there shall thy hand lead me, and thy right hand shall hold me.
If I say, surely the darkness shall cover me; even
the night shall be light about me.
Yea, the darkness hideth not from thee; but the night shineth as the day:
The darkness and the light are both alike to thee."

Transgressing air traffic control

One of my deacons constantly wanted to agitate me and was a constant "thorn in the flesh." One Sunday morning after service he again succeeded in disturbing my spirit, and when I tried to prepare for the evening service, nothing would come together. My spirit was too disturbed so I decided to take the afternoon off and go flying. I had the airplane parked at a ranch not far from Lake Kyle which was in a game reserve.

The area was not only a game reserve but also fell under the air traffic control zone. I had to have clearance from ATC. When I tried to radio them I could not obtain reception. Well thought I, I'll fly anyway keeping low so that I would not get into the path of any air traffic and keep to the rural, bush area. Right here I was breaking two laws:

1. Flying without clearance in controlled air space, and
2. Flying below 500 feet in a game reserve.

On approaching Lake Kyle I saw a guy enjoying his Sunday afternoon, doing some fishing. In the middle of the lake some fishermen were in a boat. My agitation gave way to some humor as I decided to play a joke on them. With the sun behind me, I cut the engine and dived in silence to the man on the bank. Some 50 yards/ meters above him the engine roared to life. I will never forget his face, as he looked back and ducked for cover. The guys in the boat had nowhere to take cover. I did a fly past and waived at them with both my hand and wings. On arriving home, I found I now had peace of mind and could again get in touch with God and prepare for the evening service.

All was well till later the week. My little bout with harmless fun was turned into mighty big trouble. A messenger from the court knocked on my front door and asked if I were the owner of an airplane registered as ZS APN. I affirmed and was promptly served with an affidavit accusing me of five offenses. Each offense carried $2000 fine or five years in prison! My deacon rival was now driving a number of nails into my coffin!

This all happened as we were leaving Fort Victoria for Cape Town, South Africa. Yan, his family and mine all left and I laid over a week to wait for the trial. Prayer was now the order of the day and the night. Court day arrived; I was found guilty on all five counts and received an unrealistic fine of only fifty whole dollars! Praise God from whom all good blessings flow!

"The Name of the Lord is a strong tower. The righteous run into it, and they are safe."

Unfortunately "the fat lady had not yet sung!" More trouble lay ahead. To re-enter South Africa I had to have my aircraft's annual check renewed which meant I had to occupy the services of a South African engineer, fly all the way out of South Africa to where my aircraft was. This would cost thousands of dollars and I plainly did not and never would have it. So problem solved, I would fly anyway and hopefully customs and immigration would not know of it. On angel wings I cleared both customs and flew to Sabie where I had built a hanger. I would meet the family and leave the aircraft there.

On arrival down in the Cape we found an adorable house against the mountain slope overlooking the picturesque town of Gordons Bay. Our house overlooked False Bay and every night the sun set behind

Table Mountain. More correctly, we did not find it. Yan found it and had plans of making it their home. They were so kind in giving us first choice and he and Bessie (Elizabeth) moved into an apartment. Thanks to you all, Yan, Bessie, CJ and Reynette.

The adage says "You cannot hide from the long arm of the law" and one day the phone rang and I was confronted by the Superintendent of aviation regularities in Pretoria. He inquired as to where the aircraft was, did I have the aircraft inspected and cleared for entry into the country, and so on. Again, I was in the mire of quicksand. He said if I wanted to resolve this problem without the law I should come see him. This necessitated a journey through the length of the country and back again. An appointment date was set. Again I shifted gears into Prayer and faith. Prayer first and then faith for Jesus said: *"When you pray, believe that you receive it and you shall have it."* I remember stepping physically on my Bible and saying to God: *"Lord, I don't mean to be disrespectful to your word but I am standing on your promise that whatsoever things you bind on earth (physical) shall be bound in heaven (spiritual) and whatsoever things you loose on earth shall be loosed in heaven."* I took my God given authority, loosed this occasion of fret, worry and fear and believed God would make a way.

So, I began my Mount Carmel prayer session and seeing the cloud as a man's hand (meaning we should pray until we've prayed thru until we feel the release of the Spirit.) After that it is futile to pray again. That is unbelief. Now we are to shift into faith mode which means we purposefully and manually drive away all fear out of our heart and mind. Now we rest in God for the Bible says:

"There remaineth therefore a rest unto the people of God" Hebrews 4:9 and again Jesus said: *"My Peace I give unto you, not as the world giveth, give I unto you, Let not your heart be troubled, neither let it be afraid." (John 14:27)*

So I walked into his office, said I'm sorry, apologized and begged his pardon. He smiled across the table to me and said: "OK—you are pardoned don't do it again!" The long trip was worth those words. I am glad to say today that at 72 years of age having spent 24 years in America, I have a clear record both criminal and driving. The same can be said for South Africa for 47 years (except one).

So let me tell you of my one criminal record in South Africa.

We go back to shortly after Cornelia and I were married and settled in Nelspruit in the lowveld. I loved Nelspruit because of its tropical climate. Trees, flowers and birds abound in great profusion. We rented a home out in the country and liked it very much. Only problem was it was a bare shell and we would have to supply the conveniences. No electricity, so we would use a generator. Neither was there any cabinet where I could put my revolver under lock and key, which was the law in South Africa.

My next best option was to inform our helper where we kept it and as she was the only other person in our house, she would be kept responsible should the firearm be lost. One morning as we were making up the bed we missed the revolver. It was no longer under the mattress. So it was also evident why it was now the third day that the helper did not come to work. I did not know where she lived, but I did find her. She was a young girl of about seventeen. After much persuasion I learnt that she had given it to the gardener who needed it to shoot his school principle. I rushed to the school, met with the principle and shared the news. Again, it was learned that the kid had not been at school for a number or days. Another child however came to me and said he knew where he was and would lead me there. These were black areas and not really safe to be. The kid pointed to a shack and said "He's in there!" The door was locked so I promptly smashed it down. The eighteen year old tried to escape but I caught him in an alleyway. He said he did no longer have the revolver as he had given it away. I took him to the police and they secured my revolver. I was glad to retrieve it. Later when Cornelia and I wanted to immigrate I had to obtain proof of my criminal record for immigration into America. It was then that I learned that I had a record of "negligent loss of a firearm." It was strange to me because I was never informed about this and neither ever appeared in court. I suppose the police just tagged me with it.

1976-1977

A house built on faith

In 1974 I resigned my pastorate in Fort Victoria, Rhodesia and together with Yan Venter and his family we moved down to Cape Town to do evangelistic work. We were accompanied by Br. Rock Hudson and his family. Yan and Rock being an excellent singing team had been in music and singing ministry in our church at Fort Victoria. We found homes in the picturesque town of Gordons Bay where we headquartered our newly formed evangelistic organization. God soon joined us with an excellent band and our singing ministry now comprised a drummer, lead, rhythm and base guitars, pianist, two male and two female singers. I would do the preaching, Yan would be the organizer and he inherited the grand title of National co-coordinator. Yan did a good job and soon we were ministering in churches, halls, stadiums, and theaters. After years of evangelizing— we had a great revival in a town called Caledon. It was here where my Hitchcock family had its roots. My grandfather, Boy Hitchcock was an extremely well-known figure and my father and uncle were born and raised in this little town of some 3000 people. They were all members of the staunch Calvinistic Dutch Reformed Church. Pentecostal churches were viewed as a cult of sickness. So here comes Evangelist JDS Hitchcock advertising as the grandson of the now deceased well known auctioneer, sworn appraiser and lawyer with the same initials JDS Hitchcock nicknamed (Oom Boy.) It was a great town shaking revival with many saved, baptized and filled with the Holy Ghost with the evidence of speaking with other tongues. This was completely out of doctrine to that of the Dutch Reformed Church. The Dutch Reformed Church was up in arms and described by my uncle Jean saying he knows nothing about what's being fought about, but everybody even wants to throw fists. Well, we had now formed a body of young believers and they had to be led, taught and nurtured. So Yan became the pastor. Our group disbanded and I was by this time disillusioned with the Cape weather. They say it's like a baby—either plagued with a wind or wet. Winter months of May thru August the Cape experiences soft continuous rains and come September through to December the South-Easter blows your brains out of your head. I had trouble just trying to think. January thru April is gorgeous! So we shut shop and my ex-wife, daughter Galilee and I decided to return to the good old Transvaal where the weather is equal to the best in any part of the world. I had one problem though. I did not want to live on the Rand with its great bustling cities of many millions of people. I wanted to live in the Bushveld—home of big game, birds and nature at its best.

This character streak of mine has probably been my greatest downfall in the ministry. I have avoided the cities and preferred the little towns. Making money has never been an issue to me so how could I have become a great well known evangelist if I did not haunt the places where people and money were to be found? Nevertheless, I have always first sought the Kingdom and its righteousness and so God has always added unto me the necessities and yes sometimes the luxuries of life. The only time I have really been depressed in the ministry was when I pastored the Norwood Full Gospel Church of God, in the heart of Johannesburg's elite suburb where the doctors, lawyers and the rich lived. I probably had the church which most of the pastors would have liked to have had. We had it all, a beautiful parsonage, and a good church where the church board wanted to give me a raise in salary ever so often. It was at this time that I bought the Cherokee ZS APN airplane and began to fly safaris. Of course I did not shun my pastoral duties, being well taught by my former pastor Tinus Cronje. Every night of the week I would visit the congregation members in their homes. From the members I received names of "outsiders" and would visit them too. Many received these visits with great gratitude and appreciation. They had never yet received a visit from a pastor. In my later years in America it was a cultural shock to me that people would not invite you into their home but rather stood and talked to you outside. In South Africa and Rhodesia, having knocked on a door and upon opening thereof you were immediately invited inside and a cup of coffee would always be served.

Well here I was, living in a mansion in Norwood complete with a swimming pool, an unhappy marriage so I decided to resign. Well do I remember going to see the executive board of the church and saying Brethren, I know that I haven't been in Norwood for the minimum time allotted but please relieve me as pastor of the Norwood Assembly? The Moderator asked why? Well, I said, I get up in the morning, all my people work and I have nothing to do all day. With surprise he answered, *"Brother Hitchcock, are you describing to us what heaven is like?"*

Well, they did relieve me; we rented another nice house in Norwood. I bought a Land Rover and for a time I went and hunted for a living. We had shortly before adopted two boys named Jacques and Louis. Looking back I now feel ashamed that I succumbed to the awful depression and took my three children out of the stability of Norwood Assembly. The Sunday morning that I stood up to resign a message in tongues came forth before I even opened my mouth. God said "My son, your work is not finished here." However I did resign and disobeyed God's voice and so it was that our marriage broke up in a few months. In humble, self-defense though I must say that it was partly due to the unhappy marriage which had already reached breaking point which drove me to despair, depression and destruction. After our divorce Jacques and Louis went back to their dad after some years and Galilee stayed with her mom where she graduated at a local High school.

1977

Well, having run years ahead of my story of building a house in faith lets go back to our departure from Gordons Bay. Having made plans to definitely not go to look for a house on the Witwatersrand where its populous cities stretched many miles, North to South, Pretoria to Van der Bijl Park some 70 miles and East to West, Springs to Randfontein some 100 miles, we circumvented this area. We drove east along the coast of Cape Province, Natal and headed to the Bushveld country of Transvaal and north to Louis Trichardt. Nothing came together so as a last resort we headed towards the Rand. My heart was already feeling depression. A few weeks earlier another evangelist colleague Leo Koekemoer had told me of a house at a great bargain near him in Van der Bijl Park so we decided to go and check it out. We did not like it so here we sat in our car at wits end, right in the middle of the "Rand." The word "Rand" is the Afrikaans word for Reef.

This reef comprises the worlds' richest deposits of gold, supplying some 70% of the worlds' gold and 90% of the West's gold. It runs some 120 miles, (200 kilometers) from East to West and approximately 15 to 25 miles North to South. It is peppered with gold mines.

The next day I met a realty agent named Mark. Mark was also a child of God so we "clicked" wonderfully. Later we also founded a church together and I pastored it for some months, and later found a new pastor for the church named Johan Brits.

So having said all this let's get to the story of *"the house that John built."* When Mark heard that we were looking for a house he said, "John, just this morning this property came about. I'm not sure if it will work for you. A couple has separated and they want to sell it." A while back when we were in America, God showed me a vision of a house built of stone and burned pine logs. This was our proposed *"dream house."* Mark took us to see the property which he said comprised 5 acres/2 plus hectare. When we drove down from the road we were greeted by "red hot poker" flowers and the most beautiful bushveld trees. Down the one side of the trees was a row of some 12 burned pine trees and lying on a pile was more than enough stone to build with. Although the house was exceedingly old and ugly and the barn likewise, the walls were strong and sturdy being all three foot thick and built of solid rock. There were also six strongly constructed dog kennels, and a good two roomed well-built cottage. Across the main road were also two well built "servants" cottages. The ground ran down from the road with a gentle slope and ended near a lake. The soil was rich and virgin—not a stone in it.

Behind the old house was one of the most beautiful trees I have ever set eyes upon. There were two old pepper trees and an abundance of poplars and other bushveld trees. Please bear in mind that I set store in trees than the house itself. The garden was beautiful and old ivy of perhaps 50 to 100 years old covered the walls of the old house. It was built in 1845 and I was told it was the oldest house in Johannesburg. Mark told me that the old Boer who owned it had been shot to death on the front porch by the British. This property was exactly what we wanted and dreamed of. It was a portion of the farm Hartzenbergfontein, Plot 88, and believe it or not only 17 miles from the center of Johannesburg. We had found a little portion of bushveld, right in the middle of the great cities. The little towns name was Walkerville and my address of New Life Evangelistic Outreach, P.O. Walkerville would echo through many countries of the world as my radio program expanded worldwide. From here I was within easy reach of the black township of Soweto, the Indian township of Lenasea and many colored townships. The great white churches of the entire Witwatersrand were a half to one hour's drive every which way. We were in the middle of it all and in the heart of the bushveld. When we inquired to the price, it was unbelievably low. So low in fact that I offered to pay it off in three months. The deal was accepted and signed and we moved into the cottage. Renovations would start on the house tomorrow. God is so good!

Shortly after that I met an old friend Alf Jones by name who was also saved and on fire for God. He had founded a big organization called Stepping Stones. It was a rehabilitation center, housing some 50 inmates who were off drugs and alcohol. Alf said there were many good artisans amongst them and that he would bring them to build my house. All I had to do was house and feed them, so with that said my family moved into the old house and they moved into the cottage. Within a few hours the old roof of poplar rafters and corrugated iron was torn off and the next day the plaster was stripped from the walls. As the floors were just plain dirt with linoleum placed over it all that remained now was the bare rock of the old walls. As it happened the previous owners came by and Alf said, "I will never forget his face, when he saw the house completely destroyed, and he told me to tell you that if he is not paid in three months, you will be held legally responsible and liable."

Well during the night the devil had the audacity to awaken me and reason with me. He said "John it's true you do not have a penny in your possession or any bank account—right?" I said "correct." "It's true that you do not have a single supporter—right?" Again "correct." "It's true that you do not have a single booking or meeting arranged, right?" "True." "Then why are you such a fool to destroy this house, how will you pay off the property in three months?" Didn't Jesus say: *"When a man builds a house does he not first sit and think if he has the necessary funds, lest he begins and can't finish and make a fool of himself?" (Luke 14:28-31)* You don't even have the money to feed these eight people who have come to help you. I groaned. The devil had a point so he left me to solve the problem. Well Jesus also said: *"As you believe so shall it be done unto you."* So this was to be another battle in faith. I rose from my bed and got to talking to my Master and passed on the challenge from the devil. God was quick in answering and under a heavy anointing He said: *"John, live one day at a time and the barrel will not get empty and the vats of oil not fail."* So at 4 o'clock in the morning, my ex-wife was awakened by the banging of a hammer driving a concrete nail into concrete of the wall. She asked: *"What are you doing?"* I said: *"Posting a written message from God for the devil to read and me to believe and act upon."* Our dream home was some two years in the building and sufficient unto the day was the cost and materials available every day. We did obtain a loan and paid the previous owners.

We built a large front portion onto the home which was hopelessly too big, the lounge comprising 14 x 10 meters and the office and bedroom the same. The pile of rocks were just enough to complete the house and the burnt black pine trees were cleared and oiled and supported a flat roof which caught up a tremendous amount of rain water. I intended to build a reservoir at the back and plant some crops; I unfortunately never got to it though. I became too busy in the ministry of evangelism.

Sadly though, we did not live long in this house as we accepted the pastorate in Norwood, an elite suburb of Johannesburg.

My Building Team

Before Renovation

I was told that this was the oldest house in Johannesburg and that the old "boer" farmer had been shot to death on the front porch by the British

During Renovation

After Construction

During my stay in Walkerville, my ministry expanded into a radio ministry in many countries of the world. I made the tapes in my office and would mail them to radio stations in these countries. I would conclude the quarter hour programs with the words "This then is Evangelist John Hitchcock preaching to the heart of Africa, the archipelago of the Philippines, the emerald Islands of the West Indies, Bahamas and the Caribbean, The British Isles, preaching to the heart of India, inviting you to share another quarter hour of faith, hope and love . . . ."

When we moved to the USA I again ministered on radio KGOL from Humble, Texas, which covered all of Houston and surrounding areas.

Some Radio Cassette Covers

1981

Divorce—The final decision to divorce

As mentioned earlier, I had been dating my former wife for only two months when she questioned me as to what my intentions were as to marriage. I was only 22 and naive as you ever could find. So after three months of dating we were married.

Every wife should read and practice the writing of a book called "Fascinating Womanhood" by Helen Andelin. In this book the author proves that the woman holds the key to a happy marriage. She has the power to either lock of unlock the heart of a man. By her motives, intentions and actions she can create a happy marriage or destroy it. My former wife chose the latter. Day after day, words would be slung back and forth and my stutter sure made me the holder of the shorter end of the stick! The culmination factor ends with a loss of love and respect. When this happens a marriage is doomed. Well do I remember some couple walking thru the front door of our recently built new home when the wife uttered these words with a much stressed voice. *"Oh! My, this marriage is on the rocks."* Allow me to deviate a while and come back to my story. As mentioned earlier we had moved out of our house, took the pastorate at Norwood, where after much stress and depression I had resigned, bought a Land Rover and took to hunting to feed my family. I made biltong (jerky) sold it together with the napes, skull and horns of the head. My former career as a taxidermist had trained me well for this matter. As I look back, I can see that I chose this time to be a time of getting my priorities right with God. I wanted to be alone and therefore I went hunting alone. One can imagine the odds that are against you when you have to drive the vehicle yourself, hold the spot light with one hand and then shoot with the other, a futile impossibility! Added to the above was the extreme danger of being killed and hunted myself. I was hunting in a war zone. I was on the border of Namibia and Angola where South African forces were battling the Communist army of Angola and Cuba their alliance. I was a sitting duck in the midst of this but, never ever being one to possess fear, and intelligence for that matter I didn't care.

My only companion was my little dog Injah—a Cairns terrier. Shortly before I left, I had detected a very tiny white pimple on the inner bend of my knee. It was very painful. The breaking news on TV was that there was an invasion into the area of a spider that had the configuration of "hour glass" on its body. I suppose I had been bitten by one of these, perhaps the dangerous Black Widow!

My journey from Johannesburg to the north of Namibia was a 2000 mile trip and during the time getting there, this little white pimple had grown to a ravenous sore. It resembled a boil with some twelve heads. A very painful wound indeed, covering more than a square inch. This was bush country—no hospitals, no doctors, no pharmacies so I just had to make good and do as best I could. During each day I was walking some 15 to 20 miles each day and this wound being on the bend of the knee was very painful indeed.

Having no pain killers which in any event have never worked for me, I made good by tearing a shirt and bandaging my knee very tightly. It gave some relief and also kept the dirt of the African bush out of the raw wound. Not once did I think that I could very easily have paid for this futility with my life. I had traveled 2000 miles and I had a family to feed. I did the skinning, cutting and drying of the meat all by myself. On a second trip a friend accompanied me which simplified and helped matters greatly. The Bible says: *"one putteth a thousand to flight but two putteth ten thousand to flight."*

Now let me get to my story about Injah and then return to the divorce.

On our way home to Johannesburg I was driving the entire length of Namibia which being a barren desert country, one would drive many miles without a trace of civilization. Game and carnivorous beasts were plentiful and their eyes highlighted the night in the glare of the headlights so often.

At one spot on this dark night I had stopped to check the load. Injah had taken her little walk and when I resumed my journey I had forgotten to put her in the car. En route I listened to a tape of Jimmy Swaggart being about an hour and a half in essence and on completion

I suddenly remembered I had left Injah along the road. Fear struck my heart and I turned back immediately. Where would I find her? There were many of these "turn offs" off the road. It was night and I had not been noticing the road at all. The road was as straight as a beam. This main artery thru Namibia was not asphalted, but made and covered in salt, nevertheless a very nice road indeed. I had now embarked upon an impossible situation. The glows of eyes were everywhere, I had not noticed the time or distance while traveling. But Praise God to cut a long story short, about an hour and a half later, I sort of recognized the turn off and exiting thereat, here was my black little Injah sitting waiting for me. What fear must she have harbored in her heart that night? This country was full of the carnivorous species. It was a most happy reunion! Shortly after returning home I again accepted another pastorate down at Sabie and during my visits to town Injah would ride on the back seat of the motorcycle and would always wait unleashed outside the door of the store that I visited.

Oh Lord has mercy, what must the people have thought of the new pastor with the black little dog on the back seat of his motorcycle!

Now let's get back to the final decision to divorce. For some or other reason, my ex-wife had not joined me down at Sabie. I had put her and the three children in a very nice apartment overlooking Victoria Lake in Germiston. I had a Cherokee six seater airplane, so commuting back and forth was not a problem. They were within walking distance from Rand Airport.

On one of these visits I went by car and arriving before she returned from work I went up to the apartment with my overnight suitcase, fully intending to "spend the night" as always. I was in for a big surprise. My ex-wife came from work and was not a happy camper to find me there! Following some rash words, she threw my suitcase over the wall from whatever floor she was living on and in no uncertain terms I was ushered outside of the door.

So without a word of goodbye to my children I went down, scraped together the clothes which burst out of the suitcase, got into my car and intended to spend the night in my car. It was now already dusk. It was now already dusk. After some time she came down with something resembling a branding iron and informed me that should I not leave immediately, my car would suffer the brunt of her anger. I knew she fully intended to do what was stated so without further delay I got my red Volvo sport out of there. Where to now? Well, a good friend of mine Pieter Fourie, a sergeant in the South African police force, whom I had led to Christ had an apartment in the police complex. He had left his key in a hidden place and being away from home, said I could use the apartment. I resolved to go there. It now being dark, my lights were on. The Volvo had a problem with the dip switch. Sometimes when you were required to dim your lights, they would dim and then go back to bright. Dim again and perhaps go back to bright a second time.

So when I dimmed my lights to the car in front of me, the above occurred. This obviously angered the occupants who happened to be three male and one female. Given the experience which had happened a half hour ago, my emotions were stressed to the highest breaking point. The car came behind me and began tantalizing me with dim, bright, dim, bright, etc. It was obvious they were challenging me and looking for trouble. I had passed my fortieth birthday and they were in their mid-twenties. I could both see and smell trouble coming. I could not lift a hand to my wife but here could be a fight and I was ready and eager for it.

My mom had given me her little .25 Brownie pistol and I placed this in my shirt pocket, an action that either saved my life or protected me from severe harm that night. At the first red light (robot) they came alongside. My Volvo was a left hand drive and his car a right hand. We were less than a yard/meter apart. I asked him, "What's your problem man?" "You're my problem" he retorted and got out of his car, smashing his door into my freshly painted car and took a swing at me through the window. It is so ironic that a man has always got to back down to the weapon of a woman—the tongue and the weapon of a man (his fists) he cannot use. But this was a different scenario. I exited my car with meaning and began to employ my old boxing skills. Allow me to list that in my boxing days. I had participated in 21 tournament fights, won 19, drew one and lost one and that to a future South African Olympic champion. This fight was to be the first fight after interval when I would change into my boxing attire. Upon commencement I found all the laces knotted on my boots, and trying frantically to loosen them amidst the cries of "Hitchcock—hurry up your opponent is in the ring waiting! Get in here!" So I suppose I was emotionally unprepared and lost that fight.

In the street that night however, I quickly gained the upper hand mastering with left jabs, hard right crosses to his face, ducking under his shots and landing heavy body blows. I really cannot remember even receiving one blow. His face already was a bleeding pulpy mess. He began hysterically calling his friends to bring the karate stick, which is some device with two sticks connected together with a chain. I have no idea how it is used. All I knew was that three against one with that weapon they were now brandishing was at my severe disadvantage and said: "Oh so you want to use weapons do you—well let's do it." It was then that I pulled out my Brownie .25 pistol and shot against an electric sub house. The bullet ricocheted, much to my favor and advantage. As one man they turned in their tracks and retreated to their car not without the help of the point of my shoe landing very hard kicks to their backsides. The fight ended abruptly, the cars separated and I drove on to Piet Fourie's place.

Once in bed I began weeping bitterly praying "Oh my dear God, what's happening to me? I must surely be backslidden. My marriage is disintegrating and tonight I got into a street fight. Somebody could have gotten killed!" I wept and wept which swept away the pent up anger and emotions. God has always been my closest companion. "He is a friend that sticketh closer than a brother." Early in my Christian life I had learned to trust and lean on him in everything. This was one more time.

I had been praying a long, long time, "Lord should we divorce?" It's no use carrying on. Our marriage is beyond repair. That night I said to God that it was now or never, TONIGHT I WANTED A DEFINITE ANSWER. I wanted to hear from God in no uncertain terms, John, yes divorce or John, no don't divorce.

I am going to open the Bible and I want God to speak to me with a "Yes" or a "No." "No half measures." God had already talked to me 25 times but tonight I was willing to accept the 26th time as final. I lay on the bed and started waiting for God. It was not long ere His blessed presence filled the room. Again, as always He was so near—tears gushed out of my eyes and rolled down my cheeks. As peace settled in my heart, and as His presence filled me, I waited for the answer. Out of the morass of the cares of this life, as you would show a movie film in reverse, a portion of scripture suddenly stood out of the waters—Without a shadow of doubt I knew that the spirit had given me it to read. Here was the yes or no to my divorce.

With great expectancy I turned to

"Let the woman learn in silence with all subjection, but I suffer not a woman to teach, nor to usurp authority over the man, but to be in silence." *(1 Timothy 2: 11, 12)*

This was the portion God gave me, but with vexation of spirit I closed the Bible and said: *"Oh God, I know that that portion refers to women, but I only want a direct "yes" or "no."* God's Spirit suddenly arrested me and said, *"That is your answer, read it again."* Again, I turned to the verse and read it carefully. Suddenly the Spirit of God brought another verse to my mind: viz. *"Can the leopard change his spots, can the Ethiopian man change his skin—and can your wife change her nature?"* Suddenly a great truth dawned upon me—Here laid the very crux of our whole unhappiness for 20 years. I had to confess— *"No, Lord, nobody can change the natural self. Twenty years have proved that!"*

"Then you have your answer," said God. THAT WAS IT. I was resolved to let the divorce go through. It was her who was divorcing me anyway. She had already rejected seven offers of reconciliation—now I felt at peace—the matter was finished. To have no guilt conscience, I decided to give her everything which we had built up over 20 years, except my very personal items. In the preceding six months, I had gotten into very serious financial trouble and a debt in the bank amounted to many thousands of Rand. This I would take upon myself. God would help me to pay it. He would give back to me the years which the locust had eaten. I would again sometime get back onto my feet, with another house full of furniture and perhaps God would this time give me a home, not a house, and perhaps the wife that I had been seeking for so long who would love me and fill the vacuum. It is sad when a marriage fails, and I strongly condemn the modern trend of entering into holy matrimony with a wait and see attitude. A little down the road when things get rough, the modern crowd just splits and each goes his own way. My family example and training was not so. They all stuck for life, and so it was a sad and painful experience when my former wife and I parted after 20 years, 2 months and 2 days.

This was an intense time of prayer and seeking the face of God and the resultant guidance of God is chronicled in another book I have written called: "***Divorce—Sunrise or Sunset.***" It was painful to leave my adopted daughter Galilee and two adopted sons Jacques and Louis. Needless to say, I remained faithful with my parental financial support.

Life just disintegrated during this time. We had resigned our church and I had resigned from the ministry. I began to distribute a newly formed and published Christian magazine and so spent many lonely days and nights driving and sleeping in my car. I had no stable environment and no friends. It was painful to distribute a magazine that carried articles of preachers whom I knew well and had conducted many revivals in their churches.

Here I was, exonerating their ministries, while hardly being paid anything and living in my car. God had pushed my life and ministry to the back burner. Still, I was receiving prophecies of a new and greater life and ministry.

1983

Saved by a flat battery

I am currently reading a book written by Billy Graham entitled "Angels." It so vividly describes the duties of angels on behalf of believers. In all the years I have always prayed to God the Father and Jesus Christ our Lord, and have thus received my answers to prayers from them. I have seldom thought any about these messengers sent from the presence of God to help us in our daily lives. The Bible says:

"He will command his angels concerning you to guard you in all your ways." (Psalms 91:11)

Again, the Bible states angels are ministering spirits SENT FORTH to minister for them who shall be heirs of salvation.

"Are they not all ministering spirits, sent forth to minister for them who shall be heirs of salvation." (Hebrews 1:14)

I believe that when we reach the other side beyond the veil of death, we will be fully surprised when we learn about the numerous times that angels were commanded and sent from the presence of God to protect and help us. With this in mind, it may be that angels saved five lives when we were encountered with the problem of a flat battery.

On this occasion I and four others, namely Yan Venter, his brother Nick Venter, my brother Tony and his brother in-law Joe Venter flew to Sun City. The occasion was the world title heavy weight fight between the South African Gerrie Coetzee and Mike Weaver.

En route we experienced bad turbulence and I displayed some bad piloting skills in neglecting to change fuel tanks, and so when the tip-tank ran out of gasoline/petrol and the engine abruptly stopped in midair. There was sudden pandemonium amongst all passengers.

I remember quickly changing tanks, pumping the throttle viciously and starting the engine again. Tony probably got the greatest fright of all for I recall Joe teasing him long after the incident saying "Tony wanted to open the door saying—I got to get out of here!" I recall Tony exiting the aircraft upon landing and screaming to some guys more than two hundred yards away that he will never ever get into an airplane again! He was clearly acting in shock.

Well, we were all greatly disappointed when our local champion Gerrie Coetzee failed to win the world title, but we did enjoy visiting Sun City with its neighboring Lost City. They were built and owned by the same builder and owner of "Atlantis" in Nassau, Bahamas.

Aeronautically speaking Sun City is near to our destination of Baragwaneth Airport. Actual flight time would be no longer than forty minutes. When we arrived at the airplane we found the battery to be flat. It was a beautiful sunny morning with not a cloud in the sky, so there was no need for a weather check. For some reason which I do not recall we were low on gas/petrol. There was sufficient to reach home but not for any deviation.

We spent our time idly chatting waiting for someone to arrive who would be able to supply a jump start. I think it was a Sunday morning so nobody was in any hurry of leaving. A couple of hours passed before we managed to start the engine and get underway. This lapse in time was a God send. It was still early in the morning and it was a very calm, flight. The earth had not yet heated to cause any turbulence. Without a cloud it was a perfect day for VFR (visual flight rules) flying. I do recall being concerned about the amount of fuel in the tanks, and after this experience I always made very sure I had more than enough in.

About halfway to our destination in Johannesburg we were confronted with a rather eerie sight of some hovering UFO's. On nearer approach they were found to be hot air balloons hovering somewhere between Pretoria and Johannesburg—probably over Grand Central Airport.

The next sight I saw was "bone chilling" to say the least, for low on the ground within the horseshoe circle of the Magaliesberg mountain range was a low layer of mist. It seemed like the whole area from Pretoria to way south of Johannesburg was all covered in mist. The only visible sight was the Brixton tower which indicted exactly where Johannesburg lay beneath the mist. Baragwaneth Airport would be some seven miles to the South West. The fuel level was now also a concern. With perplexity which only I was aware of, I turned toward the airport expecting to find it completely covered in mist. Great, was my relief when I found the southern end of the runway to be mist free and so I was able to land, apply full brake pressure, and come to a stop within the mist. Had the battery not delayed our departure, we would surely have encountered a total landing impossibility with insufficient fuel to deviate to another airport.

Psalms 121

*"I will lift up mine eyes unto the hills, from whence cometh my help.
My help cometh from the Lord, which made heaven and earth.
He will not suffer thy foot to be moved:
He that keepeth thee will not slumber.
Behold, he that keepeth Israel shall neither slumber nor sleep.
The Lord is thy keeper: the Lord is thy shade upon thy right hand.
The sun shall not smite thee by day or the moon by night.
The Lord shall preserve thee from all evil: he shall preserve thy soul.
The Lord shall preserve thy going out and thy coming
in from this time forth, and even for evermore."*

Piper Cherokee 260

A close call with ZS-APN

I had upgraded to a Cherokee 260 six seater and wanted to fly photographic safaris. On one such trip, we were scheduled to fly from a Safari Lodge called Thorny bush to the town of Sabie where we would overnight. Fees were paid and I had important business to finalize. My group had gone into the Kruger National Park and was scheduled to be back in time to fly and reach our destination before dark. This was unfortunately not the case. They arrived late, but I figured we still had enough time, but took the precaution to liaise with some friends to help me land. The short precarious ground airstrip was not lighted. I needed them to park their cars and light the field, should I arrive after dark.

A flight never felt so long to me. The sun set, darkness was fast approaching and it felt as if we would never reach our destination. As the last faint glimmer of light faded in the western sky, I saw the cars being parked to light the field as best they could. There were only about four cars, so I had to land as near as possible to the cars and on flaring out I felt a slight bump to the left. I thought I might have struck a car and quickly looked to the left. I felt relieved to see that the wing was still intact. Whilst parking the airplane, I was called to inspect one of the cars. It looked as if the hood/top was all rolled up. I was told that the left wing had struck it. I glanced under the wing and saw a large dent. Later inspection revealed that the whole main spar had been damaged. It was an intensive repair. What had actually occurred was that the wing had fortunately struck the car on the wings' underside. Had it been three inches lower, it would have struck the fore edge and most certainly have resulted in a nose dive into the ground with a ripped off wing. A fiery explosion killing all six passengers and possibly others would have been inevitable. Satan again set the trap, but with David I say, *"You rescued me from the horns of wild bulls, and when your people meet, I will praise you, Lord. Trust the Lord; you are His favorite. Let Him protect you and keep you safe."*

On another trip, I again had to make a night landing. My party of friends were in a jolly mood and were talking and joking. I remarked to them that this was only my second night landing and the first resulted in an accident. The laughter and jubilee instantly changed to silence and somberness, but soon reverted again after a perfect landing.

On another occasion when we were six passengers, laden to the extreme to which the law would allow, we landed on a short strip in the

Okavango swamps in Botswana. The bush camp owner told us that just the previous week an aircraft could not get airborne and had plunged right into the swamps amongst hippos and crocodiles. He was extremely nervous about our take-off. I didn't feel so good about it either and made use of every inch of runway. I told my passengers all to lean forward, revved the engine to maximum and released brake in order to gain maximum speed. I purposely did not apply flap and made use of every inch of runway before take-off. During rolling, I watched the airspeed gauge and knew that we would make it and assured my passengers of such.

Nevertheless, I did not apply flap and take off until the water's edge. The aircraft became airborne with a mighty lift off. The humor came however when one lady commented that she in her entire life would never forget the expression on the face of the camp owner. It added to the jest and humor I experienced on the previous lift off. We had cleared customs and refueled at Maun. This little town lies at the edge of the Okavango Delta and typical of Africa, the long runway was only cleared to lift off distance of the airfield. Thigh high grass covered the remaining distance which gave the impression that the runway ended where the grass began. Reflecting on hind sight, it was cruel of me not to tell my passengers that our heavy load would necessitate a roll well into the grass. Sitting next to me was a big six ft. four inch guy of 250 lbs. by the name of George. I had only met him a few hours earlier, so it was very difficult for me to contain my laughter when we invaded the grass and George added maximum stress to his seat belt, helping to enforce lift off. I later admired the floor for not expiring under the pressure of his shoes, simultaneously as panic stricken sounds of "Uh, uh, uh" escaped George's mouth.

Jacques, Louis, Galilee and my Dad

A Red Roman

Africa abounds with insects and animals. Whilst others strive for money, houses, lands, fame and fortune, I have just never had that desire. By God's goodness, I have had a considerable taste of that, but it has never been my dream to acquire such worldly heights. This desire however, has been enveloped by a love for creation and creator. So living in Africa, put me in close proximity to what and which I desired. One such account was a Red Roman.

Now what would be a Red Roman? Well, imagine a red hairy spider about 2 to 3 inches in diameter who can run about the wall of your house with lightning speed. They are said to be harmless and feed on mosquitoes, so by word of mouth, I have left them alone.

On one such occasion, I was visiting with Cornelia (before our marriage) at her parent's home. After a good Sunday lunch, I went to lie down and sleep awhile in an outside cottage. The bed was right next to the wall and not two feet from the pillow a Red Roman was perched against the wall. Gently I lay down and looking at it I remember saying aloud: *"You leave me alone, and I leave you alone—live and let live—agreed OK?"*

So with an ugly, giant, fast running spider not two feet from my face, I dozed off to enjoy a restful Sunday afternoon sleep, and sometime during this occasion I felt something heavy crawling across my face. Whether it was truly so, or whether it was my imagination in a dream, I cannot say, but one thing I can say is that, I came out, off that bed, like a cat being chased by a dog and spent some minutes trying to calm down the pulsations of my heart! Lord has mercy! Something like what the Bible says *"The wicked fleeth, when no-one persueth."*

On another occasion, I worked at a pump station on the border of the Kruger National Park. Being alone and on night shift and about 3:00 in the morning, with all reservoirs full, and nothing further to do, I decided to get away from the lights and other ambient noise, and enjoy the sounds of the African bush. This decision necessitated a climb over the fence and a walk of at least four hundred yards/meters into Africa's wildest country where the big cats still roam freely. Not only was the pump station far out in the wilds, sort of like a lonely lighthouse far away on a lonely coast, but by crossing that fence, I was now hundreds of years behind in time.

I did not have a flashlight and it was a dark, dark night with no moon or stars visible. I fingered myself around the trees and walked away into the night. At least the lights of the pump station would reveal my way back, but I did walk far enough to where they were a dim glare, and so with my back to a tree, I sat down to listen to the night, and enjoy the sounds thereof. Suddenly, I heard the snap of a twig, and as I sat quietly, I heard another, and in due process of time another. Something was coming stealthily towards me. Something was stalking me. This was not what I had anticipated. I wanted to hear the roar of the lion, some miles away. I desired to hear the call of the crickets and the frogs, the night jars or the hoot of the owl, but now I felt as though I was prey to perhaps a leopard. Suddenly further truths and realities dawned upon me. This was dry country and except for water being in the immediate vicinity, there was not any for miles around. It was obvious that I was in the heart of game concentration and in a very precarious, dangerous situation indeed. To further aggravate my fear, this sound was not receding but coming towards me! *"Serves me right,"* I thought— *"who in a sound mind would leave his job and walk into Africa's bush on a dark, black night!"* Although being only one person, on a lonely pump station, and all duties fulfilled it was still not "politically correct" to be off the job, even if there was no telephone and no communication. If this cat ate me up, who would ever know what happened to me?

Now there was only one other sound besides the stealthily stalking towards me—that being the thump of my heart in my chest! I was now wishing to be within the confines of those four walls and the comfort of the lights!

So what to do now? I decided to use the sign of my God given authority. Stand erect and with karate shout of authority run towards whatever was there. I couldn't run too fast though, because of the denseness of thorn trees.

So that is what I did, and after hearing some animal crashing through the brush, in retreat, I made a hasty retreat myself, feeling myself around the trees. Arriving back at the safety of lights and enclosure, I assured myself that the "fear of the Lord" which is the beginning of wisdom is a better choice than the fear of some carnivorous animal. Never again man!

A broken vessel renewed

"Arise: and go down to the potter's house, and there will I cause thee to hear my words. Then I went down to the potters house and behold, he wrought a work on the wheels. And the vessel that he made of clay was marred in the hand of the potter: so he made it yet another vessel, AS IT SEEMED GOOD TO THE POTTER TO MAKE IT." (Jeremiah 18:2-4)

Thank God—He never gives up on us—except for the sin of blasphemy against the Holy Ghost, there is NO sin that is not pardonable. If your vessel is cracked and broken, let Jesus fix it for you! Let Him renew your life and reinstate your dream.

<u>The Potter</u>

"The Potter saw a vessel that was broken by the wind and rain,
And He sought with so much compassion to make it over again,
"Oh I was that vessel that no-one thought was good . . ."

Remarriage

Cornelia writing: *To make this writing real you need to allow me to walk back down memory lane. How well can I recall giving my heart to Jesus at the young and tender age of five, and was privileged to have grown up in a Christian home. Thanks to God and the wonderful parents that introduced me to Him. Probably the greatest testimony any person can desire! Salvation! I continued my Christian walk and dedication to Him throughout my teenage years, very active for God all my life. I literally grew up in church! I later got baptized both in water and the Holy Ghost. I finally graduated from High School and left for college to educate myself in the field of teaching. I have to admit I've always had a desire to work for God in a full time capacity, so when it came to dating I always wanted to make sure it was Christian orientated. So during my four years of college I did not date much—concentrated on my studies and serving God.*

It was during my summer vacation at the end of my third year, 1979 that God had an appointment with me! I always returned to my home town Ladysmith to my parents for vacation. How well I recall the old time revival meetings that would go on and on for weeks on end with signs and wonders and salvation! It was in one of these meetings that God gave me a prophecy through the Evangelist John Hitchcock who was in revival at the Ladysmith Full Gospel Church of God. He prophesied the following: "I will provide your future husband at the right time and he will be in my vineyard." I knew that this "man" will be in the ministry. I remember taking that word and hid it in the secret chambers of my heart, allowing God to lead me with an open mind through my walk with Him. All good things come to an end—summer was over, I returned to college to finish my two remaining years.

After completing my studies I received my teaching post in a town called Newcastle. Finding myself not knowing a soul and on top of it I needed to find a place of worship. Recalling, I took the phone book to check all the Pentecostal churches, writing them down and starting to attend one by one till I found the right one. God was in charge and I knew He would lead me to the right place. So this particular Sunday night I walked into this Full Gospel Church of God and to say the least I found my place of worship and was happy in my teaching career. Dating, but still did not feel those "magic butterflies." Laugh out loud.

About two years into teaching my church relocated, we built a new church. This particular Sunday John Hitchcock was passing through town and being a good friend of my Pastor Yan Venter he decided to visit. Let me go back—the Saturday prior to Sunday. I had some friends over at my apartment and one of them came to me and said he feels God has something special for me in store on Sunday. I was always ready for a special treat from God! Sunday arrived and as usual I was "lost in the spirit" worshiping my God. In reverence and respect to Him I always kept my eyes closed during worship—in so doing I felt very near to God and believe that is how it should be done. Forget about any and everything, it is your time with God, and enjoy it. During the worship service my pastor welcomed his friend John in the service. When I heard it was John I reminded God of my prophecy of 1978 given to me through John that God will give me my husband. I prayed and said: "God have your own precious way." Needless to say God had another prophecy for me that morning through his prophet John Hitchcock.

John writing: It all came together one Sunday morning whilst in church with my good friend Pastor Yan Venter. During the course of the meeting I prophesied to a young lady that God was about to bring her future husband into her life NOW! Apparently I had also prophesied to her two years earlier that she need not look for a husband, but that God would send her husband to her on His time. Little did I know that I was that husband?

The following day, I was officially introduced by Yan to this lovely young lady and cupid shot the arrow. I was 43 and she 24 years of age. Due to my travels we saw very little of each other. It was before the era of cell phones and internet and communication was difficult. Due to former experiences, I was in no mood for another marriage but the more I prayed about this situation, the more I saw God leading me into a lasting relationship with her. In fact, God made it abundantly clear to me, that He would not use me again until I was married. I feel blessed and happy that God literally forced me into a relationship which ended my loneliness and brought meaning and vision into my life. Today, after 29 years of marriage, all in the ministry, I know that God went to great lengths to find the right wife for me. I thrive on instability. Life to me is the greatest when I live on the edge of danger and uncertainty. Here was a woman who would follow me literally to the ends of the earth with no assurance of where we sleep tonight, where we would eat or travel.

Cornelia and I were married on December 10th, 1983 and moved to Nelspruit, South Africa. Cornelia, being a teacher found work at the local high school and I began selling insurance and after selling four policies for which I never received any compensation, I purchased a filling station, but that was not what God intended for us. He intended for us to be back in the ministry and this is how it happened.

1985

Hitting the Oregon Trail

It was December 1984 and we were visiting with my Mom and Dad. God woke me, I rose to prayer and in one blazing moment I heard God say: *"Leave for Sutherlin in America."* I asked: *"Where is Sutherlin God?"* He said: *"In Oregon."* Well next morning, I went to the library and researched Sutherland (for that is how I thought the spelling was.) Having found none I scrutinized the map and found Sutherlin. I felt an explosion of the anointing and knew for certain—God was in this and He was leading us! I shared this with Cornelia and she became as excited as I was. We began boarding up our rental home and storing our newly bought beautiful furniture. Our furniture was exquisite and after 29 years we have never again had such beautiful possessions. Nevertheless, our hearts were ablaze with love and passion for one another and the work of God. Worldly possessions had little place in our heart and the adventure of setting out to travel distant lands was most appealing.

First duty became the ordeal of selling the business at the filling station. The idea was to sell all the gas (petrol) and then get out and so it was an inconceivable thought when God told me to fill the nearly empty tanks. *"God"* I said in exasperation—*"We're trying to obey your voice and liquidate all of this."* *"Don't argue He said, just do it."* Dumbfounded I went to the bank, loaned some money and filled those tanks to the brim, some 40,000 liters. (Jokingly) God's madness became His method that evening when the news forecaster stated that the gas (petrol) price had been increased by 25 cent a liter. With the profit we settled our debts and bought two round the world tickets, cash. We opted for this option because checking prices a Johannesburg/Portland, OR ticket round trip would cost more. So why not see the world!

We were now bound for Sutherlin, Oregon and did not know a person there and much less knew what we were intended to do. A day before we left, the old problem loomed again—no money. We set off on a world trip which would ultimately last nine months, visiting the countries of England, Holland, Belgium, Canada, America, Hawaii, Australia and Mauritius with only 150 rand in the pocket. Today the rate of exchange is eight rand to one dollar. In those days it was two rand to the dollar.

The moment we boarded the aircraft we were back in the ministry. God would open doors in the countries mentioned and so from Vancouver, Canada we boarded the Greyhound to Sutherlin, OR.

We came rolling down the Interstate 5, (the main vein from Canada to Mexico,) at 9:00PM at night when we would pass through Sutherlin. The little town of 3,800 people was so insignificant that the Greyhound didn't even stop there. The town of Roseburg, twelve miles south would be our stop of disembarkation. Like John the Baptist who doubted if Jesus was the one who should come, we also doubted if we should have been here. We prayed and asked God to confirm his leading with a mighty anointing when we saw the lights of Sutherlin. When the first lights appeared there was no anointing—the atmosphere was dead. Cornelia excused herself to head for the restroom. I knew she was going to pray. I sat dumbfounded and frozen with fear. We had $20 on us, no visa or master cards and the cheapest hotel would be nothing under $35. We had 15 pieces of luggage! We did not know a person and it was 9:00 at night and now it felt as if God had deserted us. As we passed the one and only main road thru town which contained only three stoplights, God was a million miles away—or so it felt until Cornelia came out of the restroom. As our eyes met, the anointing of God exploded and we fell crying in each other's arms. God was with us and it would all turn out OK. As we looked out the window we saw the last lights disappearing.

Little did we know that the local fair was on in Roseburg and there would "be no room in the inn" for us. Not that we had the money anyhow, but this afforded an excuse to phone a few pastors and request a nights lodging. Looking thru the phone book my eyes fell on a fellowship called "New Life," being the name of my own ministry, I decided to call it. The Pastor was very willing to pick us up and give us shelter for the night. Little did he know we only had twenty dollars on us! I still do not know how we got our entire luggage in his car.

Next morning he dropped us off in Sutherlin. I left our luggage in the foyer of a motel, left Cornelia in a restaurant (which turned out to be a bar) and proceeded to walk up the one and only main road. The town looked pretty gloomy, with so many businesses and factories closed. Vacant shop fronts were abundant and I later found out that this little lumber village was in dire straits of despair as it was cheaper to import wood from Canada than it was to harvest them at home. I remember walking past a low bed trailer and remarking to God that we would sleep under it tonight if He did not make a way for us. Here was life at the very edge of faith . . . . or was it fate? I don't think that for one moment either of us longed back to our beautiful home and furniture in the Bushveld of South Africa.

As I walked down the street I noticed a board stating Sutherlin—population—3800. Why were we here? Why have I brought my young wife out here? What was God intending to do with us? Isn't this perhaps shear madness? Well, we had already come thru England, Holland, Belgium and Canada and everyday He supplied our needs. A door would open to preach in some church and the offering would cover costs until we needed again. Those who venture into the life of faith know that God has special hand-picked helpers who know the voice of God and His leading and they are en-graced with a special love and zealousness to step in and do their share. Truly, we have very seldom mentioned our own shortage, need, and lack of inadequacy. God knows our needs and He supplies.

Walking down the one and only main street and nearing the end of town, I noticed a church and seeing nothing else of significance, I knocked on a door and the pastor opened. I introduced myself as an evangelist from South Africa and he invited me in. There were two other pastors seated. He asked me what I was doing in little Sutherlin and I responded: "Would you like to know?" He responded positively and I related how God had spoken to me and of our obedience in coming. Somewhere during the discussion he glanced at the other pastors for approval and received a wink and a "yes" nod of approval. He inquired about my luggage and I was relieved to report that it was in the hotel. To my great relief he advised that we collect it. Cornelia too was greatly relieved by the turn of events. Whilst in his office he called his wife and informed her that a couple had arrived from South Africa and he was placing them in the upper "Prophets Chamber" of the church. This room had been prepared for a missionary. Apart from the accommodation it also contained all the delicacies of food and drink. His wife rebuffed the idea of having to place the missionary elsewhere. The Pastor informed her that he knew what God was telling him to do and he planned to obey God. The missionary never arrived. The upper room we were living in truly became a "Prophets Chamber" for it was here that God revealed to us the future of South Africa. A book placed on the night stand entitled "Angels on assignment" became the source of my intense reading.

It was the story of angelic visitations and revelations to Pastor Roland Buck of Boise, ID. It created a fierce desire within me to be visited by angels and the first Saturday, in a Full Gospel Business meeting a brother told me "Brother Hitchcock, God has just revealed to me that you would soon be visited by angels," and this word began a series of revelations on the future of South Africa. In a period of six weeks God shared by way of dreams, visions and revelations the great changes which soon came to South Africa by the fall of the white Government and apartheid. On September 1st, 1985, an angel did appear, not in a body form but in strong spiritual form. I was aware of him coming through the front door of the church, up the steps, down the passage and into our room. The atmosphere was charged with intense electrical anointing. He unrolled a scroll before me and I read: (see later)

Visions regarding—Internal unrest in South Africa

The following is an extract of a tract that I distributed in South Africa.

Whilst I believe that South Africa is capable of repelling most external attacks, especially that of Black Africa, the internal unrest situation is however a different story altogether. I believe that a communist revolution is unavoidable in South Africa. Many logical arguments can be given to this question, but this is not my intention within this writing. My conclusion is derived entirely from revelations and visions from God.

The Word of God states: *"There is a God in Heaven that revealeth secrets, and maketh known . . . what shall be." (Daniel 2:28)*

"He changeth times and seasons, he removeth kings and setteth up kings—He revealeth the deep and secret things." (Daniel 2:21 & 22)

The following then is an exegesis of revelations received from God.

1. On August 28th, 1985, the following vision was revealed to me. I saw a white pumpkin (the white man's system and government) being eaten within by black worms (internal black unrest.) The total inside was eaten away and the worms crept out of the skin and crawled away. The pumpkin, having no core left, fell flat in the form of a map of South Africa and South West Africa. As the pumpkin disappeared into the earth, new shoots came up, but they bore black pumpkins (black government.) I beheld that as the black pumpkins lay in the sun, they burst open and the fowls of heaven came and ate the pips. This would tend to reveal chaos, disorder and anarchy in the country.

2. On September 1st, 1985, and angel of the Lord appeared unto me. He had a scroll in his hand and having opened the scroll I read the following words

South Africa: past and present

From a distant land my people (French Huguenots) came to this land to escape persecution, but alas, even here they were persecuted and could not live according to their precepts.

Behold I placed the white man in this country in order that he might bring the light to the dark continent, but in this calling, he has failed miserably and instead has become materialistically minded.

In confirmation of the above my wife and I asked God to give us a dream on the same night.

3. On September 11th, 1985, I dreamed I was busy explaining to someone, how I make a decision. In my dream I said to him that I would list the pros and the con's alongside each other and would thereby weigh the one against the other. But, said I, if God shows me something, then I would scrap all other ideas and believe only what God said. At this moment my wife awoke me saying, she had just had a dream of God and revealed the following:

She dreamed that she was standing next to a river and wondered in awe at the beautiful clear water (white government.) The next day however, she stood at the same place and remarked to somebody beside her, "How can it be? Only yesterday the waters were clean and white, and now it is a raging torrent of red turbulent water (communist take-over.)

Exposition of the above three revelations—South Africa is about to fall to a communist, black nationalistic revolution.

<u>Further visions regarding internal unrest in South Africa</u>

After intense prayer with my friend, Yan Venter, who is also moved by the prophetical ministry, the following revelations were revealed to us. What was revealed to the one was confirmed to the other. I simply name myself John and him, Yan. The revelations and visions were a flowing of one into the other.

On November 17th, 1985, a thing was revealed to Yan, who saw a cracked open nut revealing the white kernel, exposed and destroyed.

Exposition: The total resistance of the country is destroyed and does no longer exist. The kernel (the white man and his system) lies exposed.

John then saw the embodiment of a very evil person with most wicked, cruel and cunning eyes, moving stealthily amongst the trees. He then walked along the beach and met with a few people gathered within the secret confines of the trees. He then delivered to them the "ways and the means" of overthrowing the country. They then in turn went and gathered others to foster rebellion, riot and revolution.

God said, "Pray against this evil influence."

Yan then saw a terrible storm brewing. People stood around outside with flimsy umbrellas, which were supposed to serve as their only defense against the coming storm. Tremendous, large hailstones began falling and the umbrellas were not capable of warding off the danger. They fell right through.

God says that the above denotes the false security of the people. They see the approaching disaster, but expect nothing. Rhodesia, at least expected it.

John saw how those whites were lying slaughtered. He saw hordes of blacks, jumping up and down with tremendous glee.

God says that we should know that even now the enemy is bloodthirsty for the blood of His church.

TONGUES AND INTERPRETATION:

'Do you know the treasures of the snow? Can you declare what lies within the heart of God? How great is His love and how wide His arm of grace and mercy? I have sent revival upon revival to South Africa but my plan was that the light should be carried to the furthest parts of the north, but this was not done. Therefore my grace will no longer be extended, but know thou this, that I am still in control of everything."

John asked God, "Lord how long, when and how shall these things happen?"

God showed him an oil pipeline with an airlock therein. When the airlock reached the mouth of the pipeline, everything ground to a standstill. He then saw how that the oil again began flowing but this time for a shining black army.

John then asked God: "Lord how long before these things happen?" God answered, "Why do you ask how long, when time has already run out and it is only my grace that is still extended."

Yan then saw an erupting volcano in the North of Africa in Libya. The red lava flowed to the tip of Africa. God then said: "It is only my hand which has stayed the flow, but for how long?" On February 12th, 1986 the following visions were revealed to me.

I saw a black African lady weeping bitterly over the body of her husband who was lying handcuffed and dead next to her. I then saw tumultuous masses of people, far more than the police force or army could ever stop, moving down Church Street, Pretoria. This was happening everywhere in the country as far south as Adderley Street, Cape Town.

So in hindsight I look back these 27 years—1985 to 2012 and see that all things occurred as God had said.

Soon I was asked by the pastor to conduct a series of special meetings. They were extremely blessed and many received words of encouragement by way of prophecies, visions and revelations. At the conclusion of the meetings a man approached me and having heard that I was from a far country and had been sent by God to Sutherlin he queried whether I felt that the meetings were the reason. I said I did not feel as such. He said he had been praying for months that God would send some outsider to solve the problem he had created. He said we should meet, and having met he explained how that he was the brother of the pastor and had split his church and took many members and started his own church. The original church of some 900 members sat in two camps of half each on two sides of the fence. There was an untold feeling of hurt and animosity not only between the brothers, and their parents, who also was in the ministry, but also among the members. Just imagine a little town of 3,800 having 900 people in fighting mood.

The brother was very humble and apologetic and sincerely wanted the matter resolved and was looking to me as the mediator of reconciliation.

Well, to cut a long story short, after three months of intervention a meeting was conducted with both churches present and the matter was resolved. This matter behooves us to realize how God's great heart of love aches, when his people are at enmity and variance. Consider that God sent me and my wife half way around the earth to rectify such a situation. During these three months a personal situation occurred, of which memories I will carry to the day of my death.

A life changing burning bush experience

During our visit to Sutherlin, Oregon, I was invited to be the guest speaker at a camp meeting. During this time Cornelia fell off a log and badly hurt her back. Sometime later we slept in a tiny, small trailer in the back yard of a brother called Stan Hokinson. It was in the tiny little town of Elkton.

During our little stay there I had the following dream. I was in some kind of dark dungeon cave and a very evil presence began pushing me back into the cave. As I retreated I passed an iron gate which slammed shut in front of me. The presence forced me further back into the cave and after five gates slammed shut in front of me, this evil presence forced me against the back door. I remember in the dream the thought came to me, that if I did not know my authority in Christ this dreadful experience would be very scary indeed.

With all space of retreat now exhausted, I decided to run through the force and so it was that as I ran I kicked the 5th gate and it shot open. Likewise the 4th, 3rd and 2nd offered no resistance. I recall that as I ran to the 1st gate I realized that if it did not open, all my victories would be in vain. As I kicked this gate it also broke open and I ran into the glorious sunlight.

At this moment I awoke out of sleep and never before or after, have I ever felt the presence, power and anointing of the Spirit in a greater measure. The "electric" pulses of the Holy Ghost flooded through my spirit in boundless measure.

The meaning of the dream was revealed to me as a renewal of my fivefold ministry that I had lost due to my divorce. My ministry of evangelism, tapes, singing albums, book writing and radio was set to continue.

During this time, I had not moved or uttered a sound. I gently laid my hand on Cornelia's back. She was sound asleep and God totally healed her in her sleep. Today I look back and see some 28 years of a resumed fulfilled ministry in evangelism, tape and book distribution, four singing and piano albums and many TV and radio shows. Besides years of radio ministry I was privileged to minister on Houston's' KGOL radio for some three years. I give to God the glory for the grace He has abundantly bestowed upon me but I reproach myself for many failures only known too well by myself.

"Now to Him who is able to do immeasurably more than all we ask or imagine, according to his power that is at work within us, to him be glory in the church and in Christ Jesus throughout all generations, forever and ever! Amen." (Ephesians 4:20 and 21)

The passing of my mother

During the young years of my spiritual life, I was greatly burdened for my parents. I knew they were not "born-again" and therefore unsaved. I spent countless hours in prayer for them. Well do I recall one whole night of prayer in a chicken pen on their farm. I prayed from early night to the morning. My passion was that my mom would be saved. Of course I spent the night feeling chicken lice crawling all over me.

One day my father called me and informed me that Mom had been struck down with a vicious stroke. From that moment she would never utter another word and half her body was paralyzed. As a result I would never have known whether she came to salvation. I do know that she never smoked or drank again. This however, would not constitute salvation. It has to come by repentance, grace and faith in the shed merits of our Lord Jesus Christ.

By a series of events God settled my mind as to her eternal destination. I wrote the event in the back of my Bible and so I quote directly from it.

April 29, 1977, 6:00AM

I have a dream of a funeral of mum and come to see a beautiful little swallow lying dead, wings outstretched on its back. I awake completely out of deep sleep. Whilst praying, I hear the voice of wings of angels, flying bringing a scroll in their hands. Unfolded, I read

Beatrix Cornelia Hitchcock
Born September 11, 1914 died October 4
This is to certify that Beatrix Cornelia Hitchcock was born a little child, lived a long life and died a child of God. Finis

All I possessed now for the knowledge of certain salvation was the fulfillment of her death. Years went by and October 4, passed every year. We now return to the former story of Sutherlin, OR.

I wanted to introduce Cornelia to the big city of San Francisco which was some 500 miles away so we set out on our trip. After completing more than three quarters of the way, I began to feel very strongly that we should turn around. The further we journeyed the stronger the obsession became. Finally we turned around and headed for home. Upon entering the house the phone rang and I was informed by my brother that Mom had suffered another two strokes and if I wanted to see her alive, I should return immediately. This was impossible. I informed my brother that mom would pass on October 4th and they should be ready for it. That day was October 1st, 1985. I went into prayer asking God that He would reveal to me the exact hour of her passing. The number four came strongly to my spirit. I informed Tony that Mom would pass at 4:00 o clock on the 4th of October.

It was devastating news to me when Tony called to say that Mom had died at 11:30 PM on October 3rd, South African time. I now had no basis of faith that Mom had died a child of God and was in heaven.

A note to you reading this book: If you, brother and sister know you are saved and have no burden for your loved ones to escape eternal hell, then your relationship with God should be severely questioned.

Again I went into prayer and a series of events were revealed to me which only God, the great mathematician could have prearranged and planned.

I was in Pacific Time in Oregon and Mom was in South African time. 11:30 PM Oregon Pacific Standard Time would be 2:30 AM, October 3rd. Which time zone did God have in mind? Both the above were incorrect so logic brought me to calculate the time on the international dateline where the new day begins. So at the International dateline time Mom died on the 4th of October. Correct so far, but what about the 4 (4 o'clock?) This did not figure. It was then that I realized we have to go to the Jewish calendar for prophecies. God never intended us to interpret prophecy on our Gregorian calendar. This is the cause for all the mistakes regarding Christ's coming, dates from Adam, etc.

Remembering that we calculate from midnight to midnight on our Gregorian calendar, and South Africa being on the same time zone as Israel I simply had to convert the time to the Jewish time of 6 PM to 6 PM. In Bible days they counted in hours. When I calculated the time as in the Bible time I came to exactly half way between the 4th and the 5th hour on October 4th, 1985, which is exactly to the minute of the 4th hour (adjustments for daylight savings time had to be included.) So when God gave me the number 4 it meant the 4th hour of God's dealing as per the Jewish calendar, calculated at the International Date-line, where the new day begins on Planet Earth.

"Precious in the eyes of the Lord are the death of His saints."

The above experience happened in Sutherlin, OR, and upon completion of our duties there we purposed to return home with a stop in Hawaii, Australia and Mauritius. I had previously arranged meetings in Australia and Mauritius. Hawaii was to be a little holiday. Again with very little money in our possession we left Portland, OR bound for

Hawaii

On arrival at Honolulu, Hawaii, we took a taxi and booked into some motel. Existing on our limited funds we did our best to enjoy this beautiful island. After several days our funds were exhausted, we moved out of the motel and had nowhere to sleep that night. I heard of a Full Gospel Business Men's meeting. I attended, hoping to sell some of my music tapes, albums and books. I was seated next to a lady and unbeknown to me, my pen moved under her papers. After the meeting she came to me and asked if the pen belonged to me. I acknowledged and she asked me where we were staying. I said we would be looking for some accommodation after the meeting. "Oh, she said. I have just the place for you." She took me to the top floor of a condominium overlooking the ocean, opened the door to a luxury apartment and said that the young man to whom it belonged had informed her that he would be spending all of December on the mainland, and should any missionaries come, she was to let them have his apartment. The key was given to me and Cornelia and we moved in, feeling very thankful and relieved. We spent the next two weeks enjoying the beautiful island of Oahu in luxury fashion.

During this time I faxed my contact in Australia, informing him that we would be arriving on the 4th of January. A few days later, I received a phone call from his secretary informing me that he had returned to South Africa and that nothing had been arranged for us. She kindly however said that we would be welcome to stay in her apartment in Brisbane, and also gave us a name and number of a contact in Sydney and so we came to

Australia

On clearing customs the officer noticed my beautiful wife and asked if she was married. She pointed to me and he exclaimed "Lucky dog!" I hastily changed into more appropriate clothes and called the number. Please remember that I had a bad stammer and I can only admire the many pastors I called seeking preaching opportunities in their pulpits. Never ever did anyone ask the very logical question of "excuse me brother, but you can't even talk, how you think you can preach in a pulpit." Those who accepted me in faith were surely surprised when a fluent torrent of anointed, eloquent word poured forth.

I had been given the name of Brother Wesscott and so I called him, explaining that my contact that should have planned meetings for me had left the country and if he could use me I would be happy to comply.

He said he was presently busy but would call back in fifteen minutes. He did call and still being busy informed me to just get on the Airport Hilton courtesy bus, go to the hotel and book in till Sunday when he and his wife would come to have lunch with us. He had fully paid the board and lodging for us. This little vacation in Sydney proved very pleasant from Wednesday to Sunday. When they came on Sunday I found myself prophesying incidences to him and his wife about their marriage and ministry. Upon completion they were ecstatic and in tears that God sent somebody who had no knowledge of their present situation that could give such direction and encouragement in their lives. It also turned out as a great surprise that God had sent to me the organizer of the Billy Graham and T.L. Osborn crusades in Australia. We ministered in a few local churches and came to Brisbane where we were grateful to live in the ladies beautiful apartment. I know that these experiences seem strange to people who could just flash a credit card or cash but we were traveling on a cashless budget and it was a great God who was caring for us daily.

A bit of dishonest humor

During one of these days we decided to use our only $5 and purchase train tickets to visit the beach. With round trip tickets in hand we boarded the train and found no enter/exit gates or conductors. Arriving at the beach we saw many topless ladies in bathing suits. This was something I had never seen in South Africa or any other country for that matter.

When we boarded the train for home, again there were no gates or conductor so we decided to see as much of the country as we could and planned to remain on the train till the last stop and then make our way back. The fact we had no money would obviously not be a problem. We were enjoying a pleasant discussion with a couple next to us—all in the English language of course. Suddenly the door of the coach opened, the conductor called out "all tickets please." We froze. When he came to us I played ignorance of the English language and spoke only Afrikaans. He questioned "where's your tickets?" "Ek weet nie wat jy van praat nie. Wat is 'n ticket?" "Tickets, tickets!" "Praat my taal, ek verstaan jou nie!" "I will take you to the police." "Ek praat net Afrikaans."

Our friends just looked out of the window and I felt so embarrassed. At the end of the route we were turned over to the Station Superintendent, and amidst much Afrikaans I let out two heavily accented words "wrong train" "Oh, what the hell he said, get on the train and go home." It was an embarrassing trip back under the scornful eye of the conductor. Dishonest—YES—but King David also feigned a mad-imbecile before Achish, King of Gath when he was in trouble.

(1 Samuel 21:10-15)

We originally planned to stay in Australia for three months and had booked our exit flight accordingly. However, we were being led of the Spirit to cut the trip short and so we planned to return to Sydney and catch the earliest flight out available. Old problem crisis again—no money to catch the bus back from Brisbane to Sydney. I tried to find a job and was invited to put in a quote/estimate to paint an apartment. I visited the apartment which was evacuated and empty. In one room however there was a chest of drawers.

I opened it and found a valid credit card with a signature which could be easily forged. In our haste to exit Australia I must admit I considered paying our fare back with this card. I have never been one to fear anything but I have always feared the law. Just one thought of spending jail time in Australia, made me leave the card right in its place.

I didn't get the painting job but I did preach on Sunday and helped a window washer clean windows. When he dropped us at the station he pressed a little something in our hand. We made it to Sydney with a little en route visit to the Gold Coast. Again "topless" was the order of the day. Who can argue that God created lovely looking trees, flowers and women? We arrived in Sydney and being in extreme haste to return home with a touch in Mauritius we visited the South African Airways office to negotiate an early return. I was anticipating trouble. In my former assembly in Norwood, Johannesburg, South Africa, I had a lady member who had children in Australia and I knew that because of the Australian embargo due to Apartheid, South African flights were only allowed once a week and she had to schedule 6 months in advance. We were now anticipating a two month early immediate excursion.

On arrival at the South African Airways Managers office we were informed that there was not one seat available for three months. I tried every reasonable appeal even mentioning that my Dad spent his whole life working for South African Airways and that he was presently the manager in Angola. Nothing could be done so we shifted into faith gear.

Sir, I replied, we are servants of God and we have got to leave. You will get two cancellations and we are scheduled to fill those seats. At that moment the phone rang and two cancellations were confirmed. With great surprise he looked at us and said: "You are very lucky." The next day we were on the airplane bound for Mauritius with only 20 Australian dollars in our possession. Before we left however I tried to contact our agent Rev. Mike Jansen in Mauritius to inform him that we would be two months earlier than scheduled and we would appreciate a pick up at the airport. We were very aware that we did not have sufficient money for a hotel for the night.

Unfortunately the telephones were down. I then contacted a mutual friend in South Africa and requested him to try and let Mike know we were on the incoming 6:00 PM flight from Sydney, Australia. Piet tried but could also not get through. It was as if Mauritius was telephonically off the planet.

Mike however was becoming increasingly concerned about his mother for the last several days and by ham radio he made contact with his mother asking her what the matter was. Oh Mike, she said. Nothing's wrong but its good you called because John Hitchcock and wife are landing at 6:00 o'clock tonight at Port Louis.

When we exited customs we were delighted to find Mike with an entourage of church members. Hastily a crusade was arranged in the City Hall. Posters and TV adverts were hastily arranged and before long I ministered on island wide television and a crusade in the City Hall and some churches. We spent a delightful two weeks with Mike and his wife Janet. I found the island of Mauritius more interesting than Oahu Hawaii. It was as if every creek was filled with Delicious Monster and Broken Heart plants. The seas were gorgeous too. After nine months we arrived back in South Africa having preached in and visited eight countries. We left with R150.00 (today $20.00 and at that time 75.00 USA dollars.) We arrived home with possibly the same.

"*These Jesus sent forth, saying, Provide neither gold, nor silver, nor brass in your purses, nor script for your journey, neither two cloths, neither shoes, nor yet staves, for the workman is worthy of his meat.*" *Matt. 10:5-10 and he said unto them, "When I sent you without purse, and scripts and shoes lacked ye anything and they said nothing.*" (*Luke 22:35*)

Show me another woman who would fit in a life and marriage like this. Certainly and surely—Cornelia was handpicked!

Seven and eight's—God's numbers of Finality And New Beginnings

Shortly after Cornelia's and my marriage on December 10ᵗʰ, 1983, we began seeing the numbers 7 and 8 in strange formations, 887, 878, 788, 877, etc. It became so apparent that we believed God was trying to show us something, but what? We settled in Nelspruit, RSA. Cornelia was teaching at the High School, I was trying to sell insurance and run a filling station. Having spent the former 12 years in full time ministry, and suffering a divorce, I did not think it possible that God would again lead us into the ministry, although that's where our hearts were. But God specializes in renovations, in rebuilding the broken down and making all things new. Just consider the chaotic earth of Genesis 1:1, of the disappearance of the dinosaurs and Neanderthal man, etc. God would again create an Adam and Eve with different DNA's to that of past species of homo-erectus homo-sapiens, etc. I was in for a great surprise!

After these clusters of numbers had been appearing to us on vehicle number plates, houses, posters, etc. for many months, we happened to sleep at a prophet of God's house and the next morning he shared a dream he experienced that night.

He said John, "I saw you preaching to a packed audience in a very large room—the number 877 was clearly printed on a banner above your head." I listened in amazement. God gave him the following interpretation and in interpreting bear in mind that in Bible numeric's the numbers 7 & 8 denote fulfillment and a new beginning.

The three figures grouped together denote the new beginning, marriage and ministry.

877—I exalt you and lift you up beyond measure for Mine own sake, for my soul doth find pleasure in thee."

8—Denotes the new beginning

7—Denotes the new marriage

7—Denotes the new ministry.

They have been fulfilled and the number 8 of new beginnings denotes a new marriage and ministry. I was astounded. Was it a mere co-incidence that Evangeline was born on 7/7/87 and Charlene "procreated" at midnight as the 7th month became the 8th?

We were instantly again recruited into the ministry when we obeyed God's command to go to Sutherlin, Oregon as written earlier on in this book. As I write this book and like to think myself as retired in good health on a boat in the Florida Keys, we have spent another 29 years in marriage and ministry. We are all precious in the eyes of the Lord! If as the Bible says. *"Precious in the eyes of the Lord are the death of his saints"* then how much more precious in His eyes are the life of His saints. Both now till eternity.

Upon entering the ministry those number clusters disappeared for many years and then suddenly surfaced again resulting in a great financial blessing from many sources.

They again disappeared for many years and now for more than the past year they have been again appearing many times more numerous than before. Even my young son Johnson of eight, just turned 9 in July (7th month) is daily pointing them out. Look Dad there's the number again.

Wow! Man, I am rubbing my palms together, anticipating what Gods' going to give. I am waiting for the big one so that I can in return bless ministries and men!

In an earlier similar event, before my divorce, the numbers 007, 070 and 700 appeared in repetitious formations.

INTERPRETATION (This was for my divorce)

007—"Yea, great was the fall of Babylon, despite the sincerity of your expectations.

070—The vision is yet for an appointed time. If it tarries wait for it, for it will surely come.

700—I will sanctify you. I'll restore you and only so if you put away petty sin. Let the integrity of your hearts be before me day and night. It is faith I am teaching you. Stay in My Word and let your prayers and supplications be **First** before Me. Learn to be sensitive and accept my discipline for **the just shall live by faith.**

My Children from my first marriage

I do indeed thank and praise God for the wonderful gift of my children. Galilee, my adopted daughter from my first marriage is married to Evangelist Gary Guess who was one of my best friends before I introduced him to Galilee. He happens to be a cousin of Elvis Presley. His father Herschel Guess, cousin to Elvis grew up as neighbors in Tupelo, Ms. Gary's grandmother was the midwife who helped bring Elvis into the world. Gary and Galilee are very powerful Evangelists. Galilee is especially used of God in the gifts of the Holy Ghost, excelling in salvation, healing, deliverance and the baptism of the Holy Ghost. She is a copy of my past ministry and I am extremely honored to receive the accolade from her as the most powerful evangelist she has ever heard. Such a compliment is all the more creditworthy as it comes from such a powerful and blessed woman of God. God continues to open doors for them across the USA and many countries of the world. They have just recently opened a church in Shelbyville, Tn. and you can visit them at their website at www. guessministries.org

Gary, Galilee, Eliel and Risja Guess

It was during a crusade I was conducting at Sasolburg, South Africa that the pastor mentioned the possibility of the adoption of two brothers, named Jacques and Louis. It was a broken home situation and the State wanted them adopted. My ex-wife and I were immediately interested as we only had Galilee, and sooner than expected they were adopted and in our house and assumed the surname of Hitchcock.

It must have been terribly hard for them when our marriage split, and I do carry regret and remorse. They were later returned to their dad and again assumed the original surname. Both Jacques and Louis have done very well in life, working good jobs—and both owning their own homes.

Louis and Jacques

Louis and Jacques with Red Volvo

John Hitchcock

My children with Cornelia

Cornelia writing: *After three years of marriage God blessed us with Evangeline, our first daughter. She was one of a twin, but unfortunately I miscarried at three months, but still carried Evangeline. What a miracle! Not knowing whether I was still pregnant I had an appointment the Monday for an ultra-sound. Low and behold we heard the heart beat! I said: "this is impossible I miscarried over the weekend!" The technician replied: "well, you must have had twins!" Thank you Jesus! She has been a delight in our home and a model child. She just completed her degree after five years and graduated from Eastern Washington University in the field of Criminal Justice. We do not know of one day of sorrow, trial or problems from her. She has diligently worked her way thru college by sometimes managing two jobs and even three. We love her dearly. Good luck on your endeavors, may God lead and guide you always, "poppie." How well do I recall the day you asked me: "mom what does "poppie" mean?" I replied; "South African name for doll." It was not long after that when I noticed on the back of her high school sweats the name printed "Poppie!" I love you girl! I still up until today call both my girls "Poppie!" It is just special.*

Cornelia writing: Charlene, our second in line was born almost three years later. Being on the road doing evangelism and being not USA citizens it was hard to obtain a physician during my pregnancy. Many a time I was asked "where are you going to have this baby?" My answer would always be: "where God wants me to have her!" We had a revival in a town called Madisonville, TN, when a lady approached me and asked the same question: "Where are you going to have your baby?" Again I answered: "where God wants me to have her!" By this time we knew it was a girl. This dear lady said she would like to take me to a maternity clinic to check it out. Well, we did, but alas! We could not afford it, but God made a way and the clinic offered us a payment plan. So at the time of Charlene's birth we lived in Cleveland, TN, and our little girl saw her first light in Madisonville, TN. How well do I recall the time when we lived in Cleveland, TN, where John worked on the diesel engine. He came home one afternoon, handing me a ticket saying: "you go to this show and enjoy it." With my heavy pregnant body he dropped me off at the movie house to watch "Pretty women" my, my, did I enjoy it and laughed so much, this poor baby inside me must have thought what is going on with my mom! Today this movie is also one of Charlene's favorites. Way to go girl, I love it! She just graduated from the same college as her sister, Evangeline, graduating in the field of Journalism in 2013 and then will complete her Dental Hygiene diploma in two years at another college.

Charlene has been an avid soccer player since her first years in elementary school, continuing as one of the stars of the team thru middle school. High school was already waiting for her where she played 2nd team her freshman year and then varsity first team from 10th grade throughout 12th grade. She also captained the team throughout these years. During high school she also played club soccer. Unfortunately the day the selectors came she was placed at left back where she never saw the ball, much less had a chance to prove herself, so doing, missing out on a full scholarship for university, but did qualify for a partial scholarship. At college she again played first team, but decided to drop it by entering her fourth year to work as hard as her sister in a job, sustaining herself. We are so proud of you "Baby Char." She obtained this name due to the fact that she was the youngest player on the soccer team and therefore was "baptized" with the name of "Baby Char," which she still goes by at the age of 22. You are the pride of our lives girl, keep-a-doing what you are, may God also lead and guide you in your endeavors. We love you very much.

Cornelia writing: Our son Johnson. In 2002 we became Foster parents and fostered many children. On one particular night late, I got a phone call from Intake for Social Services asking me to pick up this little baby. He was at the police station. My husband and I were in such a hurry to get to the police station and on arrival there the little man was smiling up at us, almost like "please take me!" Little Johnson was only six months old when we picked him up. Well, to make a long story short, we fostered Johnson for some time and bonded as a family with him right from the beginning. It was just different with him than with the others we fostered. It was if God was telling us something! When he came up for adoption we decided as a family to go for it. Through many trials and tribulations and attacks from the devil little Johnson legally became a part of the Hitchcock family. I home school the little man and he is a blessing and delight, and most certainly has the love of God in his life. Way too smart . . . . !

I would like to leave this Bible verse with all three of our children, May God abide with you, and may He lead and guide you and hold you in His arms.

"For I know the thoughts that I think toward you, saith the Lord, thoughts of peace and not of evil . . ." Jeremiah 29:11 other versions "I know the plans I have for you, that you may prosper . . . ."

As always, to my wonderful children, Evangeline, Charlene and Johnson, who are always there for me, and give me so much joy, love, caring, support, kindness, and just plain terrific times. In good or bad times, we are there for each other. Thank you for being such huge blessings in my life. With all my love, Mom

My Precious Family

A vision Cornelia had about my Volvo

Cornelia and I had just sold our house in Walkerville and we were traveling to Johannesburg, I with the Volvo in front and her following with the Station Wagon. As we entered onto the bypass around the city the road narrowed down to a two way lane over a bridge and I found myself driving very near to the wheels of a giant 18 wheeler trailer. In my trunk I had the full amount of cash money accrued from the sale of the house.

At that moment Cornelia saw a vision of my car bursting into flames and immediately prayed for me. As I looked at those rolling wheels not one meter away from me, I got nervous and decided to slack off speed and get behind the truck. As I reached the rear end of the truck, my suspension bar broke, leaving my rear axle to swing any which way. Needless to say the freeway became too narrow for my swerving, meandering car which I finally managed to bring to a stop. I would surely have careened under the tractor trailer. That day we thanked God for sparing my life, car and probably the most money we have ever had at any one time. God was so good to us.

Psalm 91

*"He that dwelleth in the secret place of the most High,
shall abide under the shadow of the Almighty.
I will say of the Lord, He is my refuge and my
fortress; my God; in him will I trust.
Surely he shall deliver thee from the snare of the
fowler, and from the noisome pestilence.
He shall cover thee with his feathers, and under his wings
shalt thou trust: his truth shall be thy shield and buckler.
Thou shalt not be afraid for the terror by night;
nor for the arrow that flieth by day.
Nor for the pestilence that walketh in darkness, nor
for the destruction that wasteth at noonday.
A thousand shall fall at thy side, and ten thousand at
your right hand; but it shall not come nigh thee.
Only with thine eyes shalt thou behold and see the reward of the wicked.
Because thou hast made the LORD, which is my
refuge, even the Most High, thy habitation;
There shall no evil befall thee, neither shall
any plague come nigh thy dwelling.
For he shall give his angels charge over thee, to keep thee In all thy ways.
They shall bear thee up in their hands, lest
thou dash thy foot against a stone.*

> *Thou shalt tread upon the lion and adder: the young lion*
> *and the dragon shalt thou trample under feet.*
> *Because he hath set his love upon me, therefore will I deliver*
> *him: I will set him on high, because he hath known my name.*
> *He shall call upon me, and I will answer him: I will be with*
> *him in trouble; I will deliver him, and honour him.*
> *With long life will I satisfy him, and shew him my salvation."*

1987

Our move to the USA

As mentioned earlier, during our stay in Sutherlin, OR, God had dealt with us about the future of South Africa. These visitations were the least to say disturbing and so we decided to leave our homeland and make America our new homeland. One night I was praying on the lawn of our home in Walkerville, South Africa, when a vision appeared to me. I saw a star in the sky and God said—That star is Fort Lauderdale—follow that star. In the vision I saw a little black haired girl with us. (Evangeline had not yet been conceived) I saw us getting into a boat and evangelizing the islands. So we began making plans to leave for America. We sold our house, furniture and car. This took many months and during this time Evangeline was born.

A visit from an angel

Cornelia writing: *All packed and ready to leave for America, we stayed with a dear friend of ours, Roxy. We had this three month old baby, Evangeline. Visas were obtained for the USA and Evangeline who was a baby in arms—too young for a passport was endorsed on John's visa.*

We slept on a mattress in Roxy's living room. Around 2am I was awakened by a presence in the room. Holy! I remember focusing on the passage leading into the kitchen and there my eyes fell on this angel standing in the door. NO words were uttered—we just looked at each other, but I could feel the presence of the Lord overwhelmingly, and just as quick as lightning the angel was gone. I woke John and shared it with him. He said: "No message—no words uttered?" I said: "No." Little did we know how real the presence of that angel would be in the future!

The next morning we boarded our plane for our first leg of our journey and landed in Italy. Waiting in line for our turn to see customs, with passports open, we were ready to explore a little of Rome while we wait for our connection flight. The moment the customs officer checked John's passport and upon checking his visa for the USA, he announced: "Your daughter is traveling illegally with you." Shocked we looked at the visa and asked him to explain. The place on the visa which indicated "bearer(s)" the "s" was crossed out so Evangeline could not travel with us! What a disaster! We were told to contact the USA Embassy. This was a Saturday—all Embassies are closed till Monday which would leave us missing our connecting flight, meaning motels and money going . . . . We obtained the number to the Embassy and decided to dial it. Low and behold someone answered on a Saturday afternoon! What a miracle! After explaining our situation to the Ambassador he said: "If you can be here in half an hour I can endorse and change your visa. I had to come into the office for an emergency." The angel of God that appeared to me was directing our paths. Wow! Did we get there as fast as we could by taxi, giving the address and said: "Drive!" We made it and John's visa was changed to "bearer(s)" and we were on our way. Thank you Jesus for ministering angels!

We left South Africa on October 4th, 1987, shortly after black Monday when the stock markets of the world plunged. We planned to first visit with Yan Venter and family in San Antonio, TX, where he was pastoring an Assembly of God church. This decision was a mistake and one of the downfalls of our life. God had told us to go to Fort Lauderdale and now we headed for Texas to fulfill a series of preaching arrangements for us. We decided to go and "spy out" Fort Lauderdale at a later time. We liked San Antonio because of its similarity to the bushveld country of South Africa and so we settled in an apartment, later moving to another.

Well, after a year we decided to ride to Fort Lauderdale and see what God would have us do there. Sad to say, the time of God's leading had passed. Our meetings in Texas were not as blessed as always and arriving in Florida we were not impressed. God sent us confusion as the whole time we were there it rained heavily. All we saw was dreaded pine trees and so we returned to San Antonio. Cornelia and I still had a return trip ticket to South Africa but I opted to go on a trapping trip to Louisiana while she and Evangeline returned to South Africa to visit with her parents and family over Christmas.

1988-1997

Trapping trip to Louisiana

I had met this Cajun guy, (let's just call him Ernest) shortly before and he had mentioned that he was well versed in trapping and invited me to join him on a trip to Lake Charles, LA. As it was December, being difficult for evangelists due to a lack of bookings what with all the programs of churches, I accepted. He and I set out and visited with his mother first. It was evident that she was a satanist and I, being a child of the light, and she of darkness, a rift in communication quickly developed. Words were not spoken but you could feel it in the air.

Ernest decided against going with me, but he said he would take me and show me where to go. We drove into the bayous and he pointed out a place where I could camp but earnestly entreated me not to camp on the water but further inland in the brush. This he said was necessary because human sacrifices were offered there and my life would be in danger. He obviously knew about satanism and was probably involved in it himself.

Well, I didn't care much about being careful and just pitched my little tent on the water's edge. For a few days I tried to do some trapping but it soon became clear, I knew nothing of the art and so promptly gave it up. Cornelia would be gone for six weeks so I decided to go on a forty day fast. I would be in camp mostly every day but did go into Lake Charles to check mail which I had re-directed. Sundays I would visit the Assembly of God church where a South African, Pastor Johnny Bosman was doing a fine job for God.

One night during prayer God spoke to me and said: *"There's going to be an attack on your life, but I will protect you."* My first thought was that it would be some activity from satanists, but God had said he would protect me so I just went right on camping where I was. The next day I went into town and returned at dusk. I had been leaving

my car at a Good Samaritan whose house was on the edge of the
woods. Because of the denseness of the brush he urged me to take
his machete to chop my way thru. My camp was approximately half
a mile away from the car. As I was breaking thru the brush wearing
only shorts and tennis shoes my eyes suddenly saw a Copper Head,
third most venomous snake in America. This was indeed a miracle in
itself as the snake blended in 100% camouflage with the surrounding
leaves, branches and undercover. What occurred next happened in a
fraction of a second. As I saw the snake it was in the throes of striking
my leg. There was no time to jump away but the pure momentum of
carrying the machete, brought it between my leg and the snake, which
in turn struck against the machete. I didn't give it a second chance but
detached its head from its body with a loud curse—SATAN! All the
hairs stood up on my body. It was a close call! The nearest hospital was
more than an hour away and I did not even know where it would be.

When I entered camp I very nearly stepped onto a huge water
moccasin—another deadly snake. This time my jump was in time
and he missed. I again killed the snake and threw it over a fallen tree
thinking that some mink or critter would take it before morning. When
morning came, I needed water, took the bucket and walked to the river.
In doing so I had to bend and half-crawl under the fallen tree. Not one
foot from my face was a snake. An unpredicted, automatic reaction
occurred and I found myself in the water, bucket and all. I had gotten
twice the fright for the dead snake which had fallen compared to the
two live ones! So I give thanks again unto God for preserving my life.

Some previous night I had been flossing my teeth and I unlatched
a gold crown off a tooth which fell right into the fire. Man, talk of a fire
being quickly broken up and dispersed! It sure happened that night. I did
find the gold cap and it still covers my tooth today, twenty four years later!

Evangeline contacts a deadly blood disease

During our stay at San Antonio in 1988, Evangeline being not two
years old became very sick. Running an extreme high temperature she
lost one third of her body weight in a few days.

We worshiped at my good friend Yan Venter's church and his
assembly was very concerned about Evangeline. We took her to

hospital and they declared that she had contracted a very serious illness where the white blood cells were destroying the red (Immune hemolytic anemia disease.)

On the fourth of fifth day after seeing her withering away in front of my eyes, I decided . . . enough was enough and tonight by the power of faith in God and promises of healing by Jesus Christ our Lord, I would reverse this status/situation. Steven and Susan Rafter from church came to pick up Evangeline and together with Cornelia they left for the hospital. I decided to spend the night in prayer seeking God's face, and wandered into the beautiful Live Oak woods behind our apartment. As I walked I could feel a continual pulling of God's presence toward my left side. I followed and within a few minutes found myself in the total presence of God. It was like Moses at the burning bush. I removed my shoes from my feet and humbly made my petition known. A great peace flooded my soul and I knew Evangeline would be just fine and returned home. What I expected to be a night of prayer turned into five minutes. As I was about to exit over the fence, I thought of how foolish I was to walk away from such a tangible presence of God. I again returned and followed the "pull" of God's presence and came again to the exact same spot where I then spent a long and pleasant time with God. This experience was repeated a third time, except that I had now sort of got to learn the path thru the trees. As I walked back I felt the presence of God pulling me to another direction and after realizing I could not find the place I again followed the "pull" of the Spirit through the woods and again landed up at the same spot. After quality time again with God I returned home.

Later when Evangeline and company arrived, she still looked as sick as ever. No medicine or treatment was prescribed, but I was at peace with God. The following day was Sunday and we went to church. Evangeline was still as sick as ever. She was just lying in the isle. During the service good sister Susan Rafter came under the power of the Spirit and came walking down the aisle speaking in tongues, laid hands on Evangeline and declared her well and free from the power of Satan.

Within minutes—I declare within minutes, Evangeline was running in the isle and in my mind I said—*"Today you can run in church all you like girl. I will not stop you."* Hallelujah! THANK YOU LORD JESUS!

In hind thought I am wondering if the blood disease was not due to an experience when she was severely attacked by a hoard of Fire ants during a weekend campout. I too have often wondered why Texans and other infected Southern States have not established a certain annual day where-in all citizens eradicate these vicious pests on their properties.

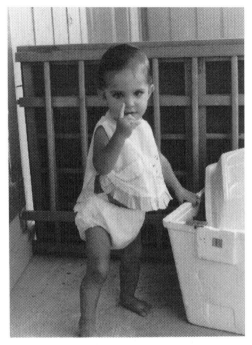

Evangeline in the early stages of her blood disease

Obtaining the Scenic Cruiser

By now I had enough of loneliness, fasting, humidity and discomfort, I decided to return to San Antonio, stopping on the way to see Pastor John McDuff whose wonderful singing, together with his brothers Roger and Coleman had blessed me since my youngest days as a Christian. I found his church and was blessed to attend a revival by Howard and Vestal Goodman. I was so blessed that I remained there until Cornelia and Evangeline returned. I had found an old Scenic Cruiser bus, bought it from John's son Gary, hired an apartment and commenced on what became a very long job of renovation and repair.

During the months of renovation God spoke to me and said: "John you missed my will at Fort Lauderdale and you will never know on this side of the grave what you missed. Go now to Tennessee and as difficult as it was to procure bookings, so easy it will be in Tennessee." Before we left for Tennessee a very fearful experience happened.

Before

During

After

Evangeline lost

Yan Venter had been visiting with us and on the morning of his departure whilst saying good buys at his car, Evangeline had been close by. When Yan left, Evangeline was gone. We searched all over—she was nowhere in the complex of apartments. Only parents who have had a missing child know the fear and worry attached thereto. When it was evident that the child was definitely lost we called the police who asked for a description of the child. They said a child had been turned in but this child had blond hair, not dark and was wearing different clothes, but they would bring the child around to us. We were beside ourselves with worry. Just imagine the relief and release of anxiety, when our one and a half year old little girl was seen—all smiles in the child restrainer of a police car. I suppose the different description was a test of identity.

What had actually happened is that Evangeline had crawled through a hole in the fence, toddled 300 yards through grass and trees came into a factory parking lot and was playing with a cat under a car where a woman found her and delivered her to the police. Lady, if you ever read this book we would like to thank you out of the depths of our hearts for finding our little girl and taken her to the police station. Thank you for not abducting her; she has been a model child and the joy of our lives.

Experiences with our Scenic Cruiser

We had worked on the Scenic Cruiser for a year and were finally ready to take to the long road with our new home—a converted motor coach. We could now evangelize as a family without the hassle of finding motels, eating in restaurants and living in church members' homes and other inconveniences. It was our first trip, traveling from Houston to Knoxville, TN The coach had a new engine inserted when it was last used four years ago. I had purposely changed all hoses to be sure that it would not leak water. There was only a heat gauge in the engine compartment, none on the dashboard. I have always had a petrified fear of overheating an engine. The devil set his snares. It was night, raining heavily and at three filling stations I pulled in, there was no water hose. Had I only pulled over and slept! Cornelia was resting in the back room (where the engine was located) she came to the front and told me she smelled something. That smell was antifreeze—unfortunately, coming from South Africa we had never used it and so did not know what it was. The coach began to lose power; I pulled over to the side of the freeway. In that pouring rain I checked the engine and very soon it become clear that this good Detroit 8V 71 diesel engine was totally destroyed and seized up. Oh what disappointment, and so much more to follow. The next day turned out to be the only day ever that I could hear the intense disappointment and hopelessness in my voice.

Charlene blinded in an accident

In 1990, shortly after Charlene's birth we lived in Cleveland, TN, where I spent four months rebuilding an engine for our Scenic Cruiser. I had to change a Detroit 8V 71 engine from a left hand to a right hand rotation. I knew very little about diesels in those days, and so it was another venture in faith. Every morning early while in prayer, God would show me what I had to do that day. Upon completion of the engine I loaded it on a heavy flatbed trailer which was hooked behind my Pontiac Grand Ville and left Cleveland and headed back to Meridian, MS with Cornelia, Evangeline, recently born Charlene and our little dog Sheba with her one little pup. Four had just died due to Sheba contacting tick fever.

En route it became clear to me that the car was not suited to pull such a heavy load. I had to keep the speed below 45mph. Near Tuscaloosa, AL, we were enveloped in a heavy downpour of rain. Suddenly the car seemed to be in better command of the load, and I increased the speed to 50mph to 55mph. Everything was planing beautiful. I feared a false illusion and decided to ever so carefully reduce speed back to 45mph. The moment I gently eased my foot off the accelerator, I lost all control. The trailer with heavy engine and radiator jack knifed, banged the side banisters and pulled the car into facing traffic, while traveling backward at 45mph. With horror I looked into the lights of an 18 wheeler just a few feet away from our car. Next our car and trailer rear ended the medium coming to rest just off the opposite freeway, this time facing with the going traffic but still opposite direction for us. Somebody got confused behind us, shot off the freeway and rear ended into the trailer. Miraculously nobody got hurt although both vehicles were totaled (meaning a write-off in South Africa.) I had slightly hurt my leg and Charlene had blood coming out of her mouth. I noted that the opposite direction of traffic in which we were traveling was backing up. Traffic in the right slow lane had come to a stop. I realized that a woman had stopped with hazard lights on. In front of her car lay the huge 18" x 18" alternator which had fallen off the trailer. I ran over and ditched it over the banisters. I will never ever forget this ladies' act of concern, placing her in extreme danger in that heavy downpour of rain on the I-20/59 freeway. No car could have cleared that heavy alternator and a multi-car pile-up would certainly have occurred. Thanks to you, Madam!

The LORD says, "I will rescue those who love me. I will protect those who trust in my name.

When they call on me, I will answer; I will be with them in trouble. I will rescue and honor them

I will satisfy them with a long life and give them my salvation."
Psalm 9:14-16 (NLT)

Later when we traveled this freeway again, I noted we had broadsided backwards thru the steepest grade of this freeway. In the middle was a deep cement gutter and our car did not overturn. How well do I recall both Cornelia and I called out at the same time, *"Jesus, help us!"*—"THANK YOU AGAIN JESUS!"

Now we come to Charlene. It was a few weeks later that we again traveled back to conduct a revival in Knoxville, TN, at a big Church of God. During this crusade while living in an apartment in the church, a horrible realization dawned upon us. Charlene was blind! Her eyes did not respond to any light, candle or flashlight. Neither did the pupils contract when we shone the light in her eyes. She was most assuredly blind.

A godly anger/wrath took hold of me. Who were satan and his principalities and powers anyway? They were defeated at Calvary, the battlefield of the gods. Jesus had defeated them there, and gained absolute authority and power saying boldly and clearly. "All power and authority is given me" and again "I give you all power and authority over the devil." TONIGHT IN CHURCH THE BATTLE WOULD BE DECIDED!

In the service I shared the incident with the people and was greatly encouraged by their concern, especially one brother who greatly favored Cornelia and me. I remember taking two chairs, sitting on the one and putting my feet on the other. I was in no way going to give any respect to the devil. I was going to talk to him in a disrespectful way. I called out loud: "Devil come here, I want to talk to you!" Under much powerful anointed command and prayer, we laid our hands on Charlene's eyes and proclaimed her well. That very night her eyes responded and she has had 20/20 vision since.

Now I know my dogma does not sound one hundred percent correct. Was it not the accident that caused her blindness? Would it not have been prudent to have rather hired a more adequate vehicle for the trip, etc.? Well, Jesus said "As you believe so shall it be." I believe the devil had a hand in that accident and placed Charlene in a position to effect the blindness. Jesus and his followers did many things that defy normality and logic—what with—rebuking storms, walking on water, shaking snakes in the fire, raising the dead, breaking the Sabbath and paying for it on a cross! Etc.

Path of our median crossing

John Hitchcock

Charlene and rattlesnakes!

During our visit and subsequent revival at Faith Tabernacle in Redding, CA, with Pastor Paul Tilley, we treated ourselves to a few days camping on the Battle-Creek River. We were cautioned that the place was a favorite haunt of rattlesnakes. It was a hot blistering day with temperature over 105 degrees. When in the vicinity of the river we were confronted with a creek which even our 4 wheel drive Jeep Cherokee was unable to cross.

Having scrounged around for some raw material to build a bridge we finally came up with a piece of corrugated iron and some logs. After some 40 minutes of maneuvering we were able to cross over, but in the event the "bridge" collapsed and on our return we would have to start all over. This event could have proved to have been one single factor in the death of Charlene or myself.

Upon arrival on the bank of the river which of necessity was a steep deep bank to the river itself, we had to descend through a boulder strewn embankment. Down at the river we enjoyed a good time of swimming, frolicking and picnicking. It was still a very hot day when we decided to head for the Jeep. Just before the ascent up the embankment we came upon a long grass, boulder strewn area, and remembering the caution of rattlesnakes, I advised the family to keep behind me in single file. For some reason Charlene came running past me and when she was some fifteen feet ahead of me suddenly the whole area began to rattle as multiple snakes sounded their warning. In my instant of assessing the situation it seemed as if at least five snakes were moving through the grass towards Charlene as she froze and stood petrified. There was only one option for me and that was to run through the snakes, whip her up in my arms and flee the area. That's what I done and thank God, I suffered no bite. Had one of us suffered a venomous bite we would most certainly have succumbed before the arduous building of the bridge over the creek and the hours' drive back to Redding. Perhaps the best deal of the experience was Evangeline's hysterical scream "satan I hate you, I hate you!" Truly Jesus said: *"Behold I give you power to tread on serpents and scorpions and nothing shall by any means hurt you."*
    (Luke 10:19)

This could have been Charlene (left) and my last day on earth. Sheba at left, Evangeline on right. Shortly before our ascent through the rattlesnakes.

Our Makeshift Bridge

Poison oak on the Big Sur

During our travels thru California, I decided to do some snorkeling on the Big Sur. Someone had warned me to be careful of poison oak, but having no former knowledge of it I did not know what to expect. So having parked on the side of the road somewhere along this marine drive which stretches from Monterey to Morrow Bay, I decided to take the family down to the ocean. It was a steep descent of some 200 yards/meters thru thick brush. I insisted that Cornelia, Evangeline and Charlene clothe themselves fully. I personally went with my snorkeling gear in hand, just wearing my swimming trunks.

Having reached the rocks down below, I donned my wetsuit, mask, helmet, fins and snorkel and entered the water. My, oh my—what cold water! I had never expected something like it. I tried my best to stay in as long as possible and see what I could beneath the waving sea grass, but after a few minutes, my body could not take it any longer and so we left.

A day or two later I experienced a tingling sensation all over my entire body which grew more and more intense. At first it felt pretty good and I wondered what these Americans were complaining about. However not long after, the tingling itch became a severe itching burning sensation. My entire body was on fire with a burning rash. From head to toe, I was covered with this poison oak infection. I never used medication or visited doctors so I just endured it. Fortunately the girls had little or no infection. After many days it finally cleared and I felt relief.

Some two years later we moved our bus to a more permanent location on David Mongers farm in Lookingglass, OR. Here we stayed for some two/three years and I would regularly mow his lawns. Well suffice it to say, I have never experienced so much poison oak. It was everywhere and I put the hand held lawnmower right thru it. I wore no protective clothing and never ever once had a recurrence of poison oak. I suppose my exceeding "overdose" had made me totally immune.

A disastrous trip up Mount Lassen.

We conducted a revival in Redding, CA, and upon leaving we were scheduled to meet my nephew Joel Hitchcock in Chicago, IL where we would minister in RV Parks and trust God to open doors in local churches. We were heading for Michigan. Again, a hot blistering day, strangers to daylight savings time we did not know that 7:00pm could be very near the hottest time of the day. Neither did we anticipate the steep climb up Mount Lassen. In hindsight we should have left 4:00 o'clock in the morning, and unhitched the car in tow. Redding lies at 555ft. ASL and as we ascended Mount Lassen which rises to 10,457 ft. ASL and somewhere midway, we encountered every RV'ers nightmare—overheating with nowhere to pull over. On the edge of the mountain pass, we pulled over on the opposite side of the road where enough space offered us a tiny space of the road. We were now on the very edge of the cliff. Thousands of feet stretched out below us. I walked back to the engine compartment and wanting to save battery power, I threw off the main switch. To my utmost horror and terror the coach with car hitched behind started rolling backwards. My beloved family and dog was inside.

Throwing the switch back on proved to no avail, so I rushed for the door where I found Cornelia already behind the wheel trying to engage the brakes, all to no avail. Again Gods great hand of safekeeping and angels who are ministering spirits to God's children came to our aid. (Hebrews 1:14) Remember, with no brakes and no power steering it was totally impossible to steer that bus. Solely by Gods' great hand the bus rolled back to the right side of the road, jack knifing the car against the cliff. Unbelievably there was no dent or the slightest damage to bus, car or trailer. The equipment however was now blocking the whole road. Shortly after a policeman arrived and as the bus could not pull itself out of the situation, he radioed for help and a wrecker came and relieved us from our problems. Some kind Samaritan had also placed water in one gallon jugs along the road so we were able to top off the water level and get to a filling station further up the pass. Whilst there and again checking on the water level, a big guy with a cowboy hat came and we talked awhile. He was a truck driver. A local resident with a home along the road also informed us that only she knew what damage that mountain had done to vehicles. If only we had remained there overnight we might have saved ourselves from much trouble further up the road. But hindsight has 20-20 vision. So we pushed on. Again we encountered overheating problems, but the summit was now very near and having no place to turn off we over-stretched the limit and probably laid the last "straw to break the camel's back."

As we descended over the summit the engine started misfiring badly and upon inspection I noticed water coming out of the left (port side) exhaust. We had either cracked the head or blown the head gasket. Fortunately a little forestry road led off the main road and we turned in there and parked some 100 yards in the forest. Now the tremendous job of removing the head and assessing the damage lay ahead of us. The family would be subjected to terrible heat in the bus. With very little space to lift the head off the blocks which in itself must weigh near 200lbs, it was an arduous task. As Murphy's Law would have it, the greater of two evils, proved to be the culprit. The head was cracked. A new one would cost more than $1000, and that was 1993. It was the long weekend of the 4th of July and we were destined to sit waiting in the veld for days before we could secure a new head. I had recently acquired a taste for Oregon wine. Oregon and Washington wines are possibly some of the best in the world. While California produces good wines they are produced in desert like soil, irrigated by snow melt in rivers coming down from the mountain ranges in the east. Fertilizer would surely be used whereas Oregon and Washington have virgin soil. So it seemed logic to me that Oregon wines would be better. Upon departing from Oregon, I went and bought a carton of twelve assorted wines and put them in the bay of the coach. Never ever before had I bought twelve bottles of wine at one time! So when the bus broke down my first thoughts went to the wine. They should not be in an evangelists coach and might be the cause of a long delay. I did not want to subject myself and family to these terrible hot conditions. Was it Gods conviction or the devils accusation? I did not feel comfortable with that carton of wine down in the bay, so I gave God the benefit of the doubt and carried the carton of the best wines in the world and put them down under a tree. There I left them, never to be retrieved again.

The next morning however, having unhitched the car, I decided to drive into Susanville and trust God that I would find a head. Sixty six miles down the road as I entered Susanville, the Spirit of God clearly spoke to me saying: "second road turn right and second house on the right." It came so suddenly that it was one movement and within seconds I stopped at the house, got out of the car and reached the front door. It happened so fast that I caught the owner sitting in his underpants watching TV. As I appeared at his open front door he whisked away to clothe himself much I suppose to the embarrassment of both of us. When he returned wanting to know how he could help me I replied "Sir, you might not understand this but God told me to consult this house. I am broken down on the mountain with a Greyhound Scenic Cruiser converted bus and need a head for a Detroit 8V71 engine. Could you help me find one in any way?" I will never forget his answer. He said: "Well, you have certainly come to the right house, I am the head of all transport in this town, but I'll tell you right off, you will not find a Detroit head here!" If only I had listened to the man and went back I would have saved so much stress, trouble and sorrow, but Oh! "Myself a fool and slow of heart to believe." (*Luke 24:25*) I decided to spend the day looking anyhow. It proved futile and I returned much discouraged to my family and broken down "home."

Hold on dear reader, keep-a-reading, a shock is still coming! Well, when the weekend passed I went to Redding where they ordered a head for me. Will I ever be able to forget the benevolence which Pastor Paul Tilley and Faith Tabernacle afforded me when they paid for the head which cost well in excess of a thousand dollars. My offerings in revivals were usually much less than that, "Faith sandwiches are thin" friend. Now the big task lay ahead. As a Detroit technician once said to me as he laid his hand on the head of my motor—"Do you know there are more than 300 moving parts in here?" That statement might be a little in excess but there sure are a lot of valves, springs, injectors and worst of all a lot of seals and gaskets which cannot move out of place. They literally lie on the engine block in a little recess. The head, having very little space between the rear floor of the bus would have to be slid over the motor thereby disrupting all the seals, etc. It was a total impossibility for Cornelia and me to lift the head and put it carefully down on its place. How could we slide the head from the side and disallow the misplacement of the tiny rubber seals. We needed a miracle!

What we did was build a ramp from logs we found amongst the trees in the forest, and with our backs bared to the direct rays of the sun in 110 degrees weather; we slid that 150 lb plus head into place! Not one seal was disturbed out of place and after torquing the head bolts it fired up perfectly. Victory and success—well partly yes but overwhelmingly NO! While we did a perfect job and never had any such problems again the great shock was about to occur.

The day I left for Susanville I told Cornelia to lock the door, close the drapes and not answer to anybody. We were parked in an extremely desolate, remote area, halfway between Redding and Susanville, a stretch of 114 miles with nothing between and well off the road. When

I returned she informed me there had been a knock on the door but she did not answer and remained quiet. The person left. So after some two weeks of sweat and severe frustration with some 2500 miles ahead of us to meet with Joel we did the last piece of work and looked up to see the big truck driver with the cowboy hat come walking through the trees. He retorted: "Hey where were you guys, I came knocking on your door looking for you, to see if I could help in any way?" I explained the situation. What he said will always carry remorse in my mind, heart and spirit. He said: "Hey, I've got a brand new head like that, still in the cellophane. You could have had it and I'd have helped you put it on." He sure was big and strong enough that with a little help from me to have placed that head squarely on its place. If only, yes if only, I had listened and responded to God and man, that day in Susanville. Too late for tears! Will we ever learn to "let go and let God." So, after all things said and done, it also did not help to sacrifice the wine either.

"Not by works of righteousness which we have done, but according to His mercy He saved us." (Titus 3:5)

Years later I passed that way again and decided to go and look for my carton of wine. They were no longer there. My oh my—what did some hunter think when he found that treasure out in the wilds, far, far away from any civilization.

A clash with Police and fire officials in the Mojave Desert

During the course of our ministry and the many miles and months of traveling through California, we endured much abuse from the authorities. Consequently California rates last in my estimation of likes amongst the United States of America. During our travels throughout America we saw the many sides of the good and the bad of the consecutive states. Concerning the two largest states of Texas and California, I noted that Texas are Texans first and then Americans. Californians feel they ARE America—period! All others states are just a trig-a-long, in their eyes.

And so it was that all over California where one would like to pullover with the coach and spend the night, which the night's stay would have to be aborted. Sometime during our sleep there would be the beam of flashlights in the bus and a pounding on the door. We were then told that we could not park here and would have to move on.

This had occurred so many times that when a similar experience happened in Mojave, I was ready to explode. We had ministered a revival in Apple Valley (of Roy Rogers's fame,) Bakersfield and Arvin. From last named Arvin at 408 feet elevation ASL to the high Tehachapi mountain range rising to 6244 feet being a mere 25 miles in distance, one could not even see the mountains because of the buildup of smoke and smog, coming from the vast cities to the South West. Wonderful California—Yea, Yea! We've all heard of the wonderful climate of southern California. What a misnomer! They mean the wonderful weather of the 20 mile diameter wide semi-circle of Los Angeles and San Diego, stretching a little to the North. Anything out of that little area is a blistering treeless desert reaching 126 degrees plus. Let's not talk about the "wonderful beaches" of California—with its COLD water reaching only 68 degrees. Let's not even talk about the gloom of mist in the San Joaquin Valley where a perpetual thick mist invades the valley for many months of the year. On the better side we will find the majestic beauty of places like the Sequoia National Forest, Kings Canyon National Park and the world beater in mountain spectacular of Yosemite National Park. Further north the Redwoods sport the world's highest 2000 yr old trees.

So it was that we came to Mojave where there was nothing except a motel and opposite it a large, I mean a very large vacant area which would possibly contain some 100 eighteen wheelers or more. Vegetation wise there was not a tree, leaf or blade of grass, only desert sand. It was late afternoon and I commenced to make a charcoal fire for our evening barbeque. Carrying out the fold-up chairs we sat down to enjoy a glass of "good" California wine whilst waiting for the coals to reach "barbeque time."

We had not sat long when the sirens of three or four fire engines came screaming along. It sounded like a very urgent situation. We got to our feet and started looking for the smoke of a fire and saw none. These fire engines were coming up the road at a hasty speed—what with lights and sirens warning the unseen traffic to "get out of the way." To our great amazement they turned right into the barren acreage, parked the engines all around us and without further ado extinguished the one foot wide smoldering coals. The boss, who seemed to be a bully of a man spoke to me as if I was a fool and questioned me insinuating

I would set the place on fire. I asked him if he thought sand/dirt could burn as there was nothing of a combustible nature anywhere that my eye could see. I further told him that I was a Safari leader to the Okavango swamps where the dry elephant grass was higher than a man and that I had a clear record of not one campfire ever getting out of control. A barrage of vocal thoughts followed and I noticed that the some fifteen fire crew was enjoying me telling him off. I wondered what they were subjected to—but the highlight came when Cornelia sitting on the buses' steps, burst into uncontrollable loud laughter telling him—"Sir you really earned your weeks' pay today." His crew had difficulty controlling their snickering.

They left and we continued the preparation of our meal on the stove inside the coach. It was now getting dark and again the outside blazed with blue police lights. A lady officer inquired saying there was a report that a man was very angry. I said "no, I'm not angry—I am bloody angry!" (A British term for extreme) I was ordered to move off after dinner. They departed. A little while later another two police cars came around. This time the officer was of a polite nature, and asked why I hadn't moved yet. I told him I was disinclined to move because I had a glass of wine, and should I be involved in an accident, I would hold the police responsible. He informed me that there was no need to move as many truckers over-nighted here on occasion and that the former lady had no authority to make me move. My anger slowly subsided and I resolved I had lost nothing in California.

Another occasion was upsetting, but I will not go into it. Suffice it to say that a police officer pulled us over whilst Cornelia was driving. She produced her South African Passport and a valid International Driving License. This insulting officer then proceeded to inform us that an International Driving Permit was not valid in California! He even said that you can only legally drive in California with a Californian driver's license!

Now you know why I previously stated that Californians think they are the entire America!

A terrifying experience with the Scenic Cruiser

It was on a trip between San Diego, CA and Yuma, AZ that we had to descend a very steep mountain pass. The coach had been newly repainted and looked great. As we began the descent I engaged second gear and proceeded slowly down. As we passed a truck run-away ramp it was a fearsome experience as the bus began to pick up speed and as much as we could apply brakes it was to no avail. Both Cornelia and I began calling "In Jesus Name—In Jesus Name!" The bus continued to pick up speed. I knew that we were now far exceeding the speed of the second gear and I began to wonder if the transmission would explode. It was now virtually impossible to successfully take the corners and I decided to ram the bus against the side banisters. With a screeching of metal against metal the speed began to decrease, until we finally brought it to a dead stop and preceded the rest of the journey very slowly in first gear. Having reached Yuma I shared my experience with a trucker who kindly checked my brakes and found the front two very poorly set and two of the four back wheels were not even connected. He adjusted the brakes and the problem was solved. Wow! Thank you Sir!

To my great amazement not even a single ding was found in the metal of the side of the bus. Only the paint was damaged which was again painted and looked as good as before. From Yuma we entered Mexico for meetings and another problem surfaced. The oil in the oil pan was increasing and getting thinner. This obviously meant diesel fuel was getting into the oil. I did not want to take chances in pushing to the next town so I decided to pull over along the side of the road and analyze the situation. Problem was though, that I had no compressor so I utilized the spare tire to pump air into the system and found that the injectors were leaking. I changed the oil and rectified the situation at the next town.

"Many are the afflictions of the righteous, but the Lord delivereth them out of them all."

Our little friend Sheba

During 1969 to 2000 I had three Cairns Terriers. The first was Blackie, who was run over by a truck. Then I obtained Injah (the one I have written about earlier) Injah died of tick fever just after I met Cornelia, and I buried her under a tree in her family's back yard in Ladysmith, Natal. The third was Sheba. They all looked identical being black in color and female by gender and I got all three as adults.

In the year of 1989 as we were getting ready to leave Pasadena, TX, with our renovated Scenic Cruiser, I noticed this little black dog in the neighbor's yard next to the church where we had a revival in Deer Park. She looked just like the other two and I wanted her ever so badly. I asked the owner of the house and she said: "Yes, please take her; I have far too many dogs."

So Sheba became part of our family for 12 years. During this time we traveled the length and the breadth of America and not once did we leash Sheba. She obeyed the spoken word and would always run exploring on her own. She always came back on her own scent—never lost once. I remember one incident when she accompanied me on a hunting trip. I had walked a good number of miles and she followed me. The next day we went hunting again and during my trip she wandered off on her own. I was not worried because she would find me, but when I crossed a path where I had walked the day before, I knew she would be confused so I sat and watched what would occur. Sure enough when she finally came and crossed our earlier crossing she stopped immediately, retreated along the paths and without much hesitation, chose the freshest one and came right up to me. My, my, my, dogs are gifted with a powerful sense of smell. Not only are dogs gifted with a sense of smell but they also know left from right. Sheba would always lie on the floor at the passenger's side.

However when we took her to South Africa, the driver's seat is on the right side and so Sheba always got in the way of brake, clutch and gas pedals, and for 9 months we could not teach her to lie on the left side. Sorry to say she hated South Africa . . . .

On another occasion we were visiting a pastor at his church with the Scenic Cruiser, as always Sheba would run around, hunting, chasing, whatsoever. So after the visit we all got in the Cruiser and took off on the freeway. After about an hour's driving we discovered Sheba is not with us. Now, we had to drive to the first off ramp and return to the church. With pounding hearts, very worried about her, but upon arriving at the back at the church we found her sitting exactly at the place where we left her. Amazing!

Our greatest gratitude toward Sheba however, was that she would never leave Evangeline when she walked off on her own. Evangeline was lost three times. The first I have mentioned earlier. The next two came later so under much perplexing worry we would walk, whistling and calling for Sheba, and so when she finally made an appearance, Evangeline would be very near. One time we found her in a water tunnel under a road. "Little blighter!"

Our final departure came whilst we were living in our coach on a church member's property. Before turning in for the night I called Sheba. She came to the door and as always she waited for the second invitation before responding. This night however she would not come in so I let her stay outside for the night. I was concerned however because we were warned about Coyotes being in the area. When the next three days passed without Sheba's appearance, we knew something had happened. Some months later the owner advised me that he knew where the remains of a dog were lying. After investigating I recognized it to be that of Sheba. That was 2000 and today 2012 her bones still lay in a cupboard in our coach. I have never been able to say a final goodbye. God rest your souls, Blackie, Injah and Sheba. Wonderful little companions you were to accompany me on my journey from earth to heaven. You will never be forgotten!

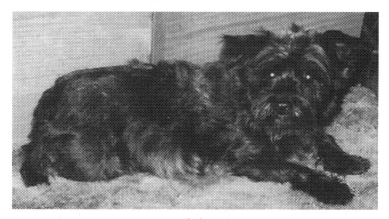

Sheba

1997

I eat poisonous mushrooms

During our stay at Lookingglass, I happened to see various species of mushrooms in abundance around our house. Being a mushroom lover I obtained a book from the library which portrayed (with photos) the good and the bad. I got the family together and with a little hand pulled cart we proceeded into the brush to enjoy a fun-filled day picking mushrooms. They were in abundance and we picked probably seven or more species. Arriving home with our mini wagon load, we got our book and divided the good from the bad. We were finally left with only one species which according to the book and photo, left no possibility or error.

Fortunately Cornelia, Evangeline and Charlene left for town and I decided to try the mushrooms. Being careful, I fried less than a tablespoon full which I thoroughly enjoyed. Within an hour I was definitely not feeling well and by the time the family arrived, I was retching violently. Together with a sample of the mushroom they rushed me to hospital and were immediately treated to a glass of charcoal fluid.

Well suffice it to say I spent the night of old year's eve 1998 in the hospital being violently ill. The sample was rushed to a mushroom expert who classified it as extremely poisonous (so much for the good book.)

I hate to think what would have happened to my family and self should we have indulged in a hearty meal. Perhaps Evangeline would have been spared as she had already stated that she would not eat mushrooms because at school she was taught that they were classified as a "fungus". As for me, if I have to abort meat and become a vegetarian, mushrooms would be my # one choice. Why . . . because

I am B-negative and come from "the hunters." I got to have meat everyday man!

Tragically my mind swept back to a story which was relayed to me whilst pastoring the church in Fort Victoria, Rhodesia. It was told that a family of Mum, Dad and four children (whom I did not know) in my former town of Sabie, South Africa, had died in hospital whilst desperately crying out "Pastor Hitchcock, come and pray for us!" Sadly, I was some 500 miles (800 Kilometers) away.

My Dad's passing

Some five months before my Dad's passing I had a dream. Someone called my name saying: *"John your Mom is on the phone, asking for you."* As I rushed to the phone I thought to myself *"this is strange because Mom is deceased,"* on answering I heard my Mom's voice as clear as it was yesterday saying: *"Johnny boy, Listen, Dad is coming to be with me. See that you are with him or else you will forever have remorse."* I said *"Will do Mom,"* and I awoke to feel God's anointing.

Some weeks later I had another dream. I saw my Dads face as it was on a rugby photo many years ago where he was in the prime of life. Over it was a banner stretched stating: "The end is near."

Well, needless to say new plans were immediately formed within our minds. We would be leaving Roseburg, Oregon, for South Africa.

Again, as always, there was no money and God would have to make a way, so we began praying and shifted into "faith gear." My only income was from preaching, and all the churches in Oregon were pretty small so offerings fitted in accordingly. Getting to South Africa now became a passion and so it was with expectancy that we traveled to Bend, OR to conduct a revival. Expectancy turned to disappointment when we left Bend and opened the envelope to see what our offering was. It was less than the cost of our fuel. A few Sundays later, I had another Sunday morning engagement and the pastor was very dubious about me coming and traveling so far, explaining that it was a very small church and the offering would not amount to much. I assured him that I had never taken money into account when preaching as my main purpose was working for God.

Reluctantly he allowed the meeting to continue. A few days later he called saying that as he expected a very small offering, he had arranged for me to preach at a Lady Pastor's church, hoping that the two offerings together might amount to something which would cover my costs. I again assured him that money was not my objective. My objective was to bring God's blessing to his church. Please bear in mind that the facts of the cost of four air tickets were never mentioned. Other evangelists can make their needs known but I could never and would not do it, the reason simply being that due to my stutter I could not make announcements. I could only preach fluently when under the anointing of the Spirit. The times when I asked Cornelia to do such favors, she always expressed her reluctance, feeling very uncomfortable about such tasks. So it was that our own special needs were hardly ever mentioned. Word of mouth via the grapevine can get around very quickly amongst pastors. I was always very careful to protect my integrity, so doing to keep doors open in the future. Sadly I must admit that the Pacific Northwest was the burial ground of my ministry. It was there that I became "burned out" and exited the ministry through the back door. If ever a need exists in the church, it would be to educate the pastors how to treat a free-lance full time evangelist.

So let's get back to the Sunday in the two small churches. We had done our best for God and His people. I was as usual moved by the gift of the Word of Knowledge and prophecy and humorously I recall a lady speaking to me after the meeting. She was a newcomer to the church and curiously she asked me "are you psychic or what?" I tried to tell her what the gift of the Word of Knowledge was all about. Bless her heart.

The lady pastor shared with me after the evening meeting that God had spoken to her when Cornelia mentioned our plans to go to South Africa, to give a missionary offering to us. She mentioned they had been saving this offering for an extended period of time and wanted to give it to our need. Suffice it to say that both morning and evening were very good offerings, much to the surprise of the pastors. Adding to this the missionary offering enabled us to buy all four tickets. We would be on our way. The time lapse between when God first spoke to us was about six months. I had been concerned that we would not make it in time but God's timing is perfect. If recall correctly, Dad passed on about six weeks after our arrival. Sad to say, due to a misunderstanding, not leaving a contact number with my wife and brother, I did miss his actual passing and my brother Tony stood in for me with prayer and Bible reading. I still carry remorse. I did however spend a few hours with his remains at the morgue and said my goodbyes and apologies. I know it will be a happy reunion when we meet on the other side.

This story cannot conclude without the following: Whilst in our coach at a revival in Selma, California, and little Charlene came to me and said "Dad there's a fox outside of the bus." Upon investigation I found a beautiful young dog. Golden in color he proved to be a cross between a Chow and either a Labrador or Retriever. After visiting all the nearby houses and farms to try to find the owner, after failure thereof we all fell in love with our new friend, Foxy. He was a wonderful pet with a warm, friendly nature. I recall one occasion when Foxy was on a bridge some thirty to forty feet above a stony creek. We were in the creek and Foxy promptly jumped off the bridge to be amongst us. We were amazed that he suffered no harm. The water was not deep enough to cushion his dive, it was boulder strewn.

Traveling North from California, we finally parked the coach on a more permanent basis near Roseburg, Oregon, at a farm in a little place called Lookingglass. It was on the property of David Monger, who lived deep in the forest. It was gorgeous to park and live amongst creeks, mountains, forests, bears, elk and deer.

Cornelia, had home schooled Evangeline for three years and Charlene for one year whilst traveling with the coach. Now the girls could attend school at Looking Glass. It was during this time that we left for the passing of my dad. After tearful goodbyes to Foxy, who would be under David's protectoral care, us four and Sheba departed for South Africa where we would be for many months ministering the Word of God.

We drove clear across the country with our Jeep Cherokee from Oregon to Delaware where we left the vehicle and Sheba with Joel Hitchcock, our nephew. They took good care thereof for us.

Whilst in South Africa we received the sad news from David that Foxy had wandered off and could not be found. On arrival back at David's place, Charlene wept bitterly at Foxy's kennel calling Foxy-Foxy.

I felt so sorry for her! We immediately set the wheels in motion to try and find him and traced his whereabouts to a nearby farm where he had been staying. The owners said that he was given to the animal shelter and when we inquired there we received the sad news that Foxy had been put to sleep a week before. Sad!

2008 TO PRESENT

Leaving the Pacific Northwest

After twelve years of living in the Pacific Northwest, of which we spent three in Roseburg, Oregon and nine in Olympia, WA we left for the South East. Our decision was influenced by the fact that Charlene, our youngest daughter had left to join her sister Evangeline at Eastern Washington University, in Cheney/Spokane, WA. We got rid of all of our "stuff," moved out of our 3500 square feet house on eight acres, packed what we thought we would need in a Ford 350 Econovan and left to find a boat. I built a double bed 18' from the ceiling and little bed for little Johnson of 5 years old. The rest of the vehicle was packed to capacity. First stop would be the girls in Cheney where we would celebrate Cornelia's birthday on October 13, 2008. The Van became our home for the next three months. Next stop was Houston, TX where auctions were due on all the salvaged boats left in the wake of Hurricane Ike. What a demolition! Debris lay everywhere! Boats were scattered on freeways and fields, houses and marinas blown to shreds. We were informed that a local apartment block wanted to give away a sailboat which came floating down the flooded street between the apartments. It turned out to be a nice 29 1/2 feet Catalina which was registered in St Petersburg, FL. How it got to Seabrook, TX is any-ones guess. However, to cut a long story short, we left it there, being unable to contact the previous owner. Nothing materialized at the auction so onward we pushed to Florida where we desired to find a boat which we would use to evangelize in the Bahamas and Caribbean islands. I was keeping good watch on E-bay as we were shopping for a boat. We kept traveling south as far as Marathon on the Florida Keys when it all suddenly came together. Hereunder follows an article I placed in an issue of the Christian Boaters Association which is self-explanatory.

In Honor of a Man of God
Our President, Pastor Marlin Simon

from Dr. John D. Hitchcock, evangethines@gmail.com

My wife Cornelia, son Johnson, and I left Washington state on October 14, 2008. We had been living in Olympia since 1999, seen our daughters through school and, as they were now away at college, we decided to begin a boat ministry to the islands.

Since 1969, I have been in full-time ministry, mostly in missionary evangelism and conducting revival crusades in churches country wide. I've pastored five churches, three in South Africa, one in Zimbabwe. My wife and I resigned our pastorate in Tacoma, WA, where we had been pastoring the local Church of God. I mention these facts to convey the point that I have met many, many thousands of pastors and Christians, but never have I met a pastor of the caliber of Pastor Marlin Simon.

Having left Washington, we spent three months traveling in search of a boat. We spent a lot of time around Houston, TX at the auctions of salvage boats which had been damaged from hurricane Ike. Nothing materialized and we headed for Florida.

By this time, my wife was pretty despondent and discouraged. All the time, we had lived in a Ford Econo van which was packed to capacity with stuff we would need on a boat. A makeshift bed was built above all and 18" from the roof. And so we travelled.

It all came together on a certain day. By a very unique set of circumstances, we met a couple by the name of Bruce and Joan DuMoulin. Over coffee, we shared our vision. These dear people called Pastor Marlin Simon, and we all met a few hours later. They had apparently not seen Pastor Marlin for some 20 years. God gave us favor with Pastor Marlin and he sent out an e-mail to the Christian Boaters Association contacts requesting a boat donation for us. It was a tremendous letter and we were overjoyed at the help and support of Brother Marlin. Nothing materialized from this, but a few days later a Baptist minister called Brother Simon informing him

that a Catholic lady was desirous to donate two boats to the ministry. Brother Simon immediately thought of us, and the next day we were standing on the deck of our 42' Uniflite power boat.

A few days later, we fired up the engines and, upon engaging gears, the water retainer hose surrounding the propeller shaft tore apart. Water now poured into the boat, necessitating a hasty haul onto dry land. I called Brother Marlin and together, with Brothers Neil Nelson and Dick Herrick, they towed our boat with a 90hp skiff to a marina. It happened to be an extremely windy day with the wind full from the front. We reached the marina at low ti'z 6pm and could not enter until high-tide, approximately 1pm, 19 hours later. The bilge pumps were working at full capacity.

Brother Marlin again returned and towed us into the marina, saving us a tremendous amount of money for towing costs. Once out of the water, Pastor Simon now came around every day and helped in many, many ways to get the boat seaworthy. Not only did he work, but he recruited as many as seven people daily to help with numerous necessities. For six weeks, they helped us daily.

Twice when my money was slow in coming through, he readily helped me with a loan, not requesting any guarantee or promissory note. He orchestrated a donation of a dinghy to our ministry. It necessitated oars and locks. He readily supplied them. Later, he supplied a sail and made the keel and rudder. Still later, he donated a 16' skiff and 88hp Johnson motor. Wow, what a gracious man of God.

I end by stating that unequivocally and emphatically I have never encountered such unselfish and determined help and support from anyone else like Pastor Marlin Simon. I am proud, as a member of the Christian Boaters Association, to be led by a person of such godly character as our President, Pastor Marlin Simon.

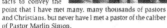

*Left to right Neil Nelson, Myself with my son Johnson,
Marlin Simon, Walt Berstler, Dick and Jeff Hale*

Our life on Southern Cross

I suppose every boater would have myriads of stories to relate, especially one who inhabits the oceans. I'll add a few which I suppose would be pretty mild in comparison.

It was on a certain day that we left for the Bentwood wreck to do some diving and fishing. Not having much previous experience with our boat, I decided along the way to first stop at White rocks. Whilst we were mooring Johnson came to report that the bedroom was under water. Upon investigation I found that the exhaust hosepipe had burst and therefore water flooded into the boat instead of exiting out of the exhaust. The bilges were at least three feet under water and as the aft stateroom is at bilge level it was as deep under sea water. Good buy new carpet!

Had we not stopped at White Rocks it is very probable that the boat could have sunken. Thank you again Jesus.

Having bilge pumped out the bilges we left the next day for the Bentwood Wreck. At the Bentwood Wreck, Cornelia and I went snorkeling. Johnson felt disinclined and rather watched us from the deck. This could have again been Gods' protection. We had not been snorkeling long when we came across an enormous Barracuda. I do not believe any Barracuda could outgrow this size and he must have been an old aggressive brute. As custom to the Barracuda they mostly lie dead still, so I watched him for a satisfying period of time, being approximately nine feet from him, and then decided to swim on past him. As I was about to lose eye contact, I felt an urge to turn on my back and face him. Having done so the brute came for me and my only defense was to lift my flippers and kick him in the face. He then turned on Cornelia who I hurriedly managed to obscure behind me, the next few moments he hovered near, eyes rotating, jaws opening and closing, baring massive teeth. Then, with much agitation, bit into the anchor rope and shook it vigorously as a large dog would shake a small animal. I signaled Cornelia and shouted to her "Let's get out of here, he has a bad attitude." Johnson watched the ordeal from the deck.

In passing I might mention, that I had once seen a documentary movie of a Barracuda biting a snorkeler in the face that died not long after. In South Africa when the Snoek run, the fishermen first club them to death outside of the boat before hauling them in. This they do due to the fact that a bite from the Snoek seems to contain blood thinner and a man can bleed profusely from such a bite. A Snoek looks so much like a Barracuda so I presume they are from the same species.

On another occasion a Barracuda was under our boat so I decided to snorkel and watch him awhile. He happened to be swimming from the bow down the port side and I was swimming up toward him. I decided to play "chicken" and see who turns out first. I remembered the bite in the face previously mentioned, so I did keep my arm in front of my face. He turned "chicken," about one yard/meter from me. I think my guardian angels have many time discussed me, saying "Man this guy is totally mad, and makes us work overtime."

During 2009 we were anchored to a large rock on the southern side of Tarpon Basin, Key Largo, FL. This rock had kept us safe from drifting through some five or six thunderstorms where gusts could reach 60 mph. By this time we felt pretty secure. On one particular night Cornelia for some reason could not sleep and was monitoring the storm and boat while I was sound asleep, so much for watching and praying. Around two three in the morning she woke me and said we were very near shore. She indicated about two feet between her hands, and when I peeked through the rear curtains we were about just that far from dangerous rocks. We were thrust into immediate panic stations; I hastily examined the situation and still am thankful to God that we did not destroy propellers and rudders.

Due to the position of the boat I could not go forward because of the anchor line, so I decided to thrust forward gear on port side, maneuvering the boat around facing shore now, throwing the boat in reverse pulling the rock behind till far enough from shore into deeper water and the rock once again anchored us till morning. Other arrangements were made and good-bye rock, thanks for past protection, but never again!

Our Boat, Southern Cross

Alligator Reef experience

We set out on this Easter weekend excursion with the boat. First we anchored at Lignumvitae Key for a few days and then left for Alligator reef.

The weather was not very cooperative, very windy and boisterous, but the Hitchcock's are out on this great adventure! With a child sea sick and everything falling we arrived at Alligator reef. Cornelia had to hook the buoy and after much stress she did it. By now her nerves were shot, she and Johnson were sea sick with everything still falling everywhere. Just there and then Cornelia said: "get me out of here please!" So we unhooked and went back to Indian Key to ride out the storm. After almost a week of horrible weather it calmed down and once again we were on our way to Alligator reef.

A few days prior to this Galilee, my daughter called to relate the following story. She said that after her meeting as she walked back to their motor coach, she was suddenly inspired to pray for me. She said her prayer became very intense and soon she was rebuking the spirit of death under a very heavy anointing. I had just had a dangerous experience so thought her prayers were directed to that occasion. Not so, it was about to happen.

As we came to the buoy at Alligator Reef, Cornelia went forward to the bow to secure the knot. I idled slowly upwind, not knowing that the current was flowing in the opposite direction and so it was that we sailed over the buoy which got stuck in the rudder and propeller. What happened next I still do not understand, but the boat changed direction, the 15' skiff came alongside and began to ram the side of the boat with extreme force! These blows came every few seconds in accordance with the waves. It was totally obvious that a great hole in the hull would follow these repeated blows.

Hurriedly I donned mask and snorkel and dived under. I did not know if I would incur a heavy fine if I just cut the rope of the buoy, so I decided to try and detach the buoy. I was now fighting a buoy which was in turn trying to pop out of the water. I became acutely aware that this was a very dangerous situation. If it moved or slipped as was my intention in maneuvering, I could be caught in the rope with no hope of survival in less than a minute. With great force I tried to unwrap it and then suddenly it shot out of the water. I came out unscathed. It could have so easily gone the other way.

Thank God that the Uniflite builders built a very stable solid boat. The incessant blows from the skiff against the hull could have sunk us. It would be extremely costly enough to lose our boats but the fine to have a sunken boat salvaged which was destroying coral reefs, I would not even like to think about.

By the law of averages, things should go well one time and bad one time, but in normal life things seem to go well one time and bad ten times. In all these dangerous experiences I've mentioned the reverse equation has been in force. Escaping death went well ten times and bad never yet. I can only give God the sincere thanks for this. It has never been my own doing.

"The name of the Lord is a strong tower, the righteous run into it, and they are safe." (Proverbs 18:10)

Storms at sea are no joke and can be terrifying for young inexperienced boaters like Cornelia and I, and Florida waters can produce some dreaded thunderstorms during summer months.

It was on one of these days, that we decided to visit a few islands in the Everglades with a friend by the name of Dennis. He, being a seasoned captain, would sail ahead in his boat and we would follow. About three miles into our journey a violent thunderstorm threatened, and we cast anchor to await the passing storm. The great cumulus nimbus thunder clouds were all around and looking back we saw an enormous waterspout exactly over where we were anchored before we left. These water tornadoes have the capability of overturning and destroying boats. If it would have had any success in overturning our solid, heavy 42' Uniflite, I do not know, but I think it would have been exciting to have been there. (The angels must have sighed with relief!)

During our anchorages on the Bay side of Key Largo at Tarpon Basin and Sunset Cove, as stated before, storms could become very severe. Tarpon Basin with a diameter of less than two miles is totally ringed and enclosed with age old Mangrove trees. Logically, this should be a very safe haven but we have experienced some severe weather on numerous occasions. On one of these occasions I had the skiff tied bow and stern to the Port side of our boat. I did this because the bilge pump was out of action, and mind you this was a new bilge pump which cost me over $50.

(God, please help me to overcome my frustration and anger at the products labeled "made in China." Some are designed to break just after the warranty expires and other are designed not to work at all.) The violence of the wind and waves and consequent whip lashing of the boat would force me to literally dive into the skiff, to manually operate the bilge pump.

On a few occasions the rope would snap and on one occasion the cleat tore right out of the boat and shot past the temple of my head, with unbelievable force and speed. The force of that cleat would have embedded itself deep into my skull.

"Some trust in chariots, and some in horses, but we will remember the name of the Lord our God. They are brought down and fallen, but we are risen and stand upright." (Psalms 20: 7 and 8)

Thank you Jesus!

A near death experience

In June of 2011 I had a very unique experience. It all resulted from my two front crowns coming loose from my teeth. As Murphy's Law would have it they came off as I was brushing my teeth and "presto" right down the drain into the bowels of our motor coach. After a long difficult search I found them, made an appointment at my dentist friend in Tacoma, WA. He did not like the idea as he put it that the teeth fell into the "sewage system" and proceeded to sanitize them for more than an hour, as best he could. We were en route to visit Evangeline and Charlene in Cheney, WA, and during our stay there I was experiencing considerable pain. An abscess had developed. Shortly before all this, I had seen a vision, different to all others I had ever seen in my life—and believe me there have been hundreds, if not thousands. All prophets who have been gifted with visions will agree that they come by way of a very clear thought or dream empowered and generated by the anointing of the Spirit and the knowledge of the presence and closeness of God.

This vision was different. I was lying awake but with closed eyes on my bed and with my eyes looking at closed eyelids, I saw my face as if in clouds. My face showed the same age as I am now and I was dead. My face then disappeared and again appeared from another angle.

This happened possibly seven times. They all signified a deceased John Hitchcock. I thought it strange. Hereafter I had a dream and dreamed I was inside a high wall as high as a tennis court fence and over the top, big black thick octopus like arms came crawling and a voice said: "The arms of death!" I called Galilee and shared the vision and dream with her. Her answer was in no ways consoling as she said: "Dad I also had a dream last night, I dreamed you were driving your car over thick roots of trees, you got bogged down and the roots engulfed the car and crushed you."

Was this the 778's I have been seeing, am I about to pass to the great beyond?

Upon arriving home I called Doc Dave who said I should come in to see him immediately. Arriving there he took one look and said "John, I give you one and a half days to live, max two. The puss in that abscess enters the sinus passages into the brain and you are gone." He placed me in the chair, took a scalpel, and opened the abscess, squeezing out the killer fluid, removed the crowns and pulled the teeth—all without tranquilizers or an injection, amidst a lot of personal squealing and groaning. Thanks to you Doc Dave for saving my life and only charging me 200 smackers for it.

My nephew—Joel Hitchcock

Today, one of the greatest evangelists I know of, both in America and worldwide is my nephew Joel Hitchcock. Seldom have I seen an evangelist who is undaunted and unafraid to call the blind, deaf, dumb and lame onto his platform, pray publicly for them and then check their healing before all present. Such is Joel.

His ministry began at age twelve when he would preach on a resort that my brother Tony was managing. He also went into the bush and preached to the trees. He later acquired a motorcycle (dirt bike) and toured halfway through the continent of Africa, preaching the good news to rural villages. He sometimes would carry a cross in several cities throughout South Africa. On one occasion he chanced upon a crowded soccer stadium in Soweto, South Africa's most dangerous and largest black area and learned that it was a communist rally. Joel entered the stadium and listened to the different speakers, including one who would later become the president of South Africa. Joel related to me that one young radical urged the youth to kill white soldiers and police and that their children would bathe in their fathers' blood. Another one recited a poem he had written about revolution and AK 47s. Eventually Joel left and then began to carry his cross outside the stadium. Suddenly he was asked by someone what he was doing, after which he was told to follow him. Joel was lead to the platform, and to his surprise he was told that he would be the next speaker. When Joel began to speak the power of God anointed him and he began exclaiming something to the effect of: "I am not here to proclaim revolution, I am here to proclaim revival and salvation through Jesus Christ. I am not here to proclaim the power of the AK47 but rather the power of the blood of Jesus etc." It was not long before the whole crowd began to AMEN him. God used this political meeting as an opportunity for Joel to share the Gospel.

So Joel's ministry has grown. He is a humble servant of God and I believe the greatest still lies ahead. You can follow him on Face Book, visit his website at www.joelhitchcock.com., and his church website at www.RiverCity.co their church's name is River City Church at 20520 Sand Hill Rd, Georgetown, DE

I am extremely humbled and thankful that Joel states that my ministry had a tremendous impact upon him in his young years.

Joel is married to Heidi and they have four beautiful children: Anthony, Rebekah, Timothy and Trey.

Joel and Galilee grew up as cousins and both have tremendous ministries.

A Ministry grows of Joel Carrying the Cross to

Caption: one of his many Mass International Crusades

Last but not least

Cornelia, my dear wife! Come December 10th, 2013 we will be married thirty years. When we married, there was a prophecy spoken over us that she was finely chosen for me. Little did she realize what she was venturing into?

Shortly after marriage, God spoke to me saying: "John I give you a choice. Do you want to be a national evangelist and on the ranks of the great national evangelists or do you want to simply travel with your family?" I chose the latter, and today after all these years, we have been together 24/7 year in and year out. When our girls left home for university, God gave us a newcomer.

It has not been an easy marriage and many would have parted years ago. Being with each other morning till evening sure has its challenges for "familiarity breeds content" and alternatively "absence makes the heart grow fonder."

She is a woman who has had no certain dwelling, has had to do without the luxuries of a dishwasher, clothes washer and dryer, microwave, etc. (for the last 5 years.) Show me one who lives in extremely humid 94 degree weather without an air conditioner, whilst going through menopause! She is one who has retired with me "in faith" with little a month as income and has to believe God for daily miracles.

Contrariwise, we have weathered the storms of life. We have learned that God is a provider and keeper in all circumstances and that we are not dependant on organization or the hand of man for our keeping. The last five years of recession has not stressed us like others. We have learned that God is truly our Jehovah Jireh (The Lord will provide,) Jehovah Rapha (The Lord that Heals,) Jehovah Tsidkenu (The Lord our Righteousness,) Jehovah Shalom (The Lord is Peace,) Jehovah Nissi (The Lord my Banner,) Jehovah-Raah (The Lord my Shepherd.)

All glory be to Him forever and ever. One prayer remains.

Even so . . . Come, Lord Jesus! *(Rev 22:20)*

CONCLUSION

And so my life's journey continues. My health and energy levels are above par to which I give gratitude and thanks to God. My greatest wish is to remain under God's faithful hand of guidance and grace.

Before I close this book, may I have the humble privilege of praying with you the prayer of repentance and forgiveness?

"Our dear God and Heavenly Father we come to you in Jesus Name and pray that you will forgive us all our sins and cleanse us in the blood of Jesus. Thank you for knocking at our hearts door. We open to you, please come in and dwell with us till eternity. Thank you God, Amen."

Contact information:
John Hitchcock
evangelfires@gmail.com
www.johnhitchcockministries.blogspot.com

I conclude this book with sincere thanks to my in laws
for the gift of their wonderful daughter

Cornelia's Parents Johan and Nellie Cronje